A FOREIGN POLICY FOR AMERICANS

A FOREIGN POLICY
FOR AMERICANS

Senator Robert A. Taft

DOUBLEDAY & COMPANY, INC., 1951
GARDEN CITY, NEW YORK

Foreword by the Author

I HAVE WRITTEN this book to emphasize the fact that the freedom of the people of the United States is in serious danger from the foreign policy of the present Administration. I have frequently written of the danger to liberty at home from the constant increase in the activity, the spending, and the power of the Federal Government, but today the threat from foreign policy is even greater. We have wandered far from its true purpose to preserve the peace and liberty of the people of the United States. Even when the purpose has been correctly understood, mistakes of judgment have led us into dangerous paths. We are embarked on a voyage at this moment in which a continued failure of understanding and judgment may wreck the greatest adventure in freedom the human race has ever known.

Our forefathers came to a continent of forests, wide plains, and savages. They lived by the work of their own hands. Those who did not wish to work for another man opened new land for themselves. There was no trace in their hard, free life of a caste system or a feudal system or an inherited aristocracy. More than a century before Marx was born a frontier equality in social relations gave us—and still gives us—an unequaled social democracy in the true sense of those Communist-perverted words. The pioneers, who carried with them one book, the Bible, also laid up for us a moral capital which has not yet been exhausted.

5

Out of this society of free men great leaders have sprung at every crisis in our history. They have resembled each other singularly. In basic qualities of profound morality, courage, common sense, and foresight Lincoln was one with Washington.

Today we face threats to our liberty and moral foundation from abroad and from our foreign and domestic programs. Distance has been so diminished by the airplane, and weapons have become so destructive, that this threat must be met on a world scale. If we are foolish in our use of our strength, we shall not survive; and with our freedom will disappear the little that remains of freedom in the rest of the world.

Power without foresight leads to disaster. Our international relations have been conducted with so little foresight since 1941 that six years after vast military victories in Europe and Asia we face a more dangerous threat than any that has menaced us before. Our soldiers, sailors, marines, and airmen have not failed us. Our political leaders have. By 1941 anyone who was not bamboozled by Soviet psychological warfare knew that the Soviet Government was a predatory totalitarian tyranny intent on establishing Communist dictatorship throughout the world. But our leaders failed to foresee that the Soviet Union would turn against us after the defeat of Germany and Japan. They made no attempt to insure our future against that eventuality. They brought forth no positive policy for the creation of a free and united Europe or for the preservation of the independence of China. They preferred wishful thinking to facts, and convinced themselves that Stalin would co-operate with them to create a free world of permanent peace. So at Teheran, Yalta, and Potsdam they handed Stalin the freedom of eastern Europe and Manchuria, and prepared our present peril.

Their foresight was such that in face of all the facts, as late as May 4, 1950, according to the New York *Times,* President Truman "asserted repeatedly that he saw no possibility that the 'cold war' would develop into a shooting war and even promised to reduce the defense budget next year."

On June 25, 1950, the Korean war began. The deaths and wounds that Americans have suffered there have at least served to educate our national Administration—after the event. It has been the most expensive education that the people of the United States have ever paid for.

What is the record?

In 1945, when Mr. Truman became President, the Soviet Union was exhausted. Much of its industry was destroyed. It had no atomic bomb, no long-range bombing planes, no serious navy. Its hold on eastern Europe was shaky. China was our ally and the Chinese Communists were hemmed into a small area.

President Truman held such power as no man had ever held before. Our air force was incomparably superior to any other. Our navy was more powerful than the combined navies of the rest of the world. Our army was a superb fighting force at the peak of efficiency. Our industrial plant, by far the greatest in the world, was intact. We alone had the atomic bomb which guaranteed the speedy destruction of any nation that might dare to risk war with us. We could have seized and held the initiative for the creation of a free and peaceful world. Our leaders did not know how or where to lead.

Today Stalin has atomic bombs and long-range bombers capable of delivering them on the United States. He has 175 Soviet divisions, and 60 satellite divisions in Europe, and a Chinese Communist army of about 3,000,000 in Asia. He has some 50,000 tanks and more than 15,000 tactical aircraft. His Indo-Chinese accomplices are draining the strength of the French Army. His guerrillas are withstanding the British Army in Malaya. He has riveted an iron control on eastern Europe. China is his ally. To face Stalin's 225 divisions the Western democracies and ourselves are scheduled to have thirty divisions in Europe—perhaps—by the end of 1951. Moreover, Soviet psychological warfare has been so successful in Western

Europe that one fourth of the French and one third of the Italians vote Communist.

In 1941 Stalin ruled 180 million subjects and was not sure that he or his empire would survive. In 1951 Stalin directs 800 million people. Unless our foreign policy is conducted more competently than it has been during the past ten years, our very survival is in doubt. There may be infinite arguments as to the wisdom of many steps in our foreign policy since 1943. But there can be little argument as to its results.

There is an old saying that the road to hell is paved with good intentions. Our national administration has had good intentions.

We do not need to seek further than the Sermon on the Mount to know the first step we must take if freedom under God is to survive in our country and in the rest of the world:

"A good tree cannot bring forth evil fruit, neither can a corrupt tree bring forth good fruit.

"Every tree that bringeth not forth good fruit is hewn down, and cast into the fire.

"Wherefore by their fruits ye shall know them."

Contents

1. What Are the Purposes of a Foreign Policy?

NO ONE can think intelligently on the many complicated problems of American foreign policy unless he decides
first what he considers the real purpose and object of that
policy. In the letters which I receive from all parts of the
country I find a complete confusion in the minds of the people
as to our purposes in the world—and therefore scores of
reasons which often seem to me completely unsound or in-
adequate for supporting or opposing some act of the Government. Confusion has been produced because there has been no
consistent purpose in our foreign policy for a good many years
past. In many cases the reason stated for some action—and
blazoned forth on the radio to secure popular approval—has
not been the real reason which animated the Administration.

Fundamentally, I believe the ultimate purpose of our foreign
policy must be to protect the liberty of the people of the
United States. The American Revolution was fought to establish a nation "conceived in liberty." That liberty has been defended in many wars since that day. That liberty has enabled
our people to increase steadily their material welfare and their
spiritual freedom. To achieve that liberty we have gone to war,
and to protect it we would go to war again.

Only second to liberty is the maintenance of peace. The

results of war may be almost as bad as the destruction of liberty and, in fact, may lead, even if the war is won, to something very close to the destruction of liberty at home. War not only produces pitiful human suffering and utter destruction of many things worth-while, but it is almost as disastrous for the victor as for the vanquished. From our experience in the last two world wars, it actually promotes dictatorship and totalitarian government throughout the world. Much of the glamour has gone from it, and war today is murder by machine. World War II killed millions of innocent civilians as well as those in uniform and in many countries wiped out the product of hundreds of years of civilization. Two hundred and fifty thousand American boys were killed in World War II and hundreds of thousands permanently maimed or disabled, their lives often completely wrecked. Millions of families mourn their losses. War, undertaken even for justifiable purposes, such as to punish aggression in Korea, has often had the principal results of wrecking the country intended to be saved and spreading death and destruction among an innocent civilian population. Even more than Sherman knew in 1864, "war is hell." War should never be undertaken or seriously risked except to protect American liberty.

Our traditional policy of neutrality and non-interference with other nations was based on the principle that this policy was the best way to avoid disputes with other nations and to maintain the liberty of this country without war. From the days of George Washington that has been the policy of the United States. It has never been isolationism; but it has always avoided alliances and interference in foreign quarrels as a preventive against possible war, and it has always opposed any commitment by the United States, in advance, to take any military action outside of our territory. It would leave us free to interfere or not interfere according to whether we consider the case of sufficiently vital interest to the liberty of this country. It was the policy of the free hand.

I have always felt, however, that we should depart from this principle if we could set up an effective international organization, because in the long run the success of such an organization should be the most effective assurance of world peace and therefore of American peace. I regretted that we did not join the League of Nations.

We have now taken the lead in establishing the United Nations. The purpose is to establish a rule of law throughout the world and protect the people of the United States by punishing aggression the moment it starts and deterring future aggression through joint action of the members of such an organization.

I think we must recognize that this involves the theory of a preventive war, a dangerous undertaking at any time. If, therefore, we are going to join in such an organization it is essential that it be effective. It must be a joint enterprise. Our Korean adventure shows the tremendous danger, if the new organization is badly organized or improperly supported by its members and by the public opinion of the people of the world.

The United Nations has failed to protect our peace, I believe, because it was organized on an unsound basis with a veto power in five nations and is based, in fact, on the joint power of such nations, effective only so long as they agree. I believe the concept can only be successful if based on a rule of law and justice between nations and willingness on the part of all nations to abide by the decisions of an impartial tribunal.

The fact that the present organization has largely failed in its purpose has forced us to use other means to meet the present emergency, but there is no reason to abandon the concept of collective security which, by discouraging and preventing the use of war as national policy, can ultimately protect the liberty of the people of the United States and enforce peace.

2

I do not believe it is a selfish goal for us to insist that the overriding purpose of all American foreign policy should be the maintenance of the liberty and the peace of the people of the United States, so that they may achieve that intellectual and material improvement which is their genius and in which they can set an example for all peoples. By that example we can do an even greater service to mankind than we can by billions of material assistance—and more than we can ever do by war.

Just as our nation can be destroyed by war it can also be destroyed by a political or economic policy at home which destroys liberty or breaks down the fiscal and economic structure of the United States. We cannot adopt a foreign policy which gives away all of our people's earnings or imposes such a tremendous burden on the individual American as, in effect, to destroy his incentive and his ability to increase production and productivity and his standard of living. We cannot assume a financial burden in our foreign policy so great that it threatens liberty at home.

It follows that except as such policies may ultimately protect our own security, we have no primary interest as a national policy to improve conditions or material welfare in other parts of the world or to change other forms of government. Certainly we should not engage in war to achieve such purposes. I don't mean to say that, as responsible citizens of the world, we should not gladly extend charity or assistance to those in need. I do not mean to say that we should not align ourselves with the advocates of freedom everywhere. We did this kind of thing for many years, and we were respected as the most disinterested and charitable nation in the world.

But the contribution of supplies to meet extraordinary droughts or famine or refugee problems or other emergencies is very different from a global plan for general free assistance to all mankind on an organized scale as part of our foreign policy. Such a plan, as carried out today, can only be justified on a temporary basis as part of the battle against communism, to prevent communism from taking over more of the world and becoming a still more dangerous threat to our security. It has been undertaken as an emergency measure. Our foreign policy in ordinary times should not be primarily inspired by the motive of raising the standard of living of millions throughout the world, because that is utterly beyond our capacity. I believe it is impossible with American money, or other outside aid to raise in any substantial degree the standard of living of the millions throughout the world who have created their own problems of soil destruction or overpopulation. Fundamentally, I doubt if the standard of living of any people can be successfully raised to any appreciable degree except by their own efforts. We can advise; we can assist, if the initiative and the desire and the energy to improve themselves is present. But our assistance cannot be a principal motive for foreign policy or a justification for going to war.

We hear a great deal of argument that if we do not deliberately, as part of a world welfare program, contribute to the raising of standards of living of peoples with low income they will turn Communist and go to war against us. Apart from such emergency situations as justified the Marshall Plan, following World War II, I see no evidence that this is true. Recent wars have not been started by poverty-stricken peoples, as in China or India, but by prosperous peoples, as in a Germany led by dictators. The standard of living of China or India could be tripled and yet would still be so far below the United States that the Communists could play with equal force on the comparative hardships the people were suffering. Communism is stronger today in France and Italy than in India, though the standard of living and distribution is infinitely better in the first two countries.

However, I think as a general incident to our policy of protecting the peace and liberty of the people of the United States it is most important that we prevent the building up of any great resentment against the success and the wealth which we have achieved. In other words, I believe that our international trade relations should be scrupulously fair and generous and should make it clear to the other peoples of the world that we intend to be fair and generous.

For the same reason, and as a contribution to world economic progress, I believe that some program like the Point

Four program is justified to a limited extent, even if the Russian threat were completely removed. I supported the general project of a loan to Brazil to enable that country to build up a steel industry to use the natural resources which are available there. I believe that the policy not only assisted the development of that country in some degree but that in the long run it contributed to the growth of trade between Brazil and the United States and therefore to our own success in that field. But such programs should be sound economic projects, for the most part undertaken by private enterprise. Any United States Government contribution is in the nature of charity to poor countries and should be limited in amount. We make no such contribution to similar projects in the United States. It seems to me that we should not undertake any such project in such a way as to make it a global plan for sending Americans all over the world in unlimited number to find projects upon which American money can be spent. We ought only to receive with sympathy any application from these other nations and give it fair consideration.

Nor do I believe we can justify war by our natural desire to bring freedom to others throughout the world, although it is perfectly proper to encourage and promote freedom. In 1941 President Roosevelt announced that we were going to establish a moral order throughout the world: freedom of speech and expression, "everywhere in the world"; freedom to worship God "everywhere in the world"; freedom from want, and freedom from fear "everywhere in the world." I pointed out then that the forcing of any special brand of freedom and democracy on a people, whether they want it or not, by the brute force of war will be a denial of those very democratic principles which we are striving to advance.

The impracticability of such a battle was certainly shown by the progress of World War II. We were forced into an alliance with Communist Russia. I said on June 25, 1941, "To spread the four freedoms throughout the world we will ship airplanes and tanks and guns to Communist Russia. If, through our aid,

Stalin is continued in power, do you suppose he will spread the four freedoms through Finland and Estonia and Latvia and Lithuania? Do you suppose that anybody in Russia itself will ever hear of the four freedoms after the war?" Certainly if World War II was undertaken to spread freedom throughout the world it was a failure. As a matter of fact, Franklin Roosevelt never dared to go to war for that purpose, and we only went to war when our own security was attacked at Pearl Harbor.

3

There are a good many Americans who talk about an American century in which America will dominate the world. They rightly point out that the United States is so powerful today that we should assume a moral leadership in the world to solve all the troubles of mankind. I quite agree that we need that moral leadership not only abroad but also at home. We can take the moral leadership in trying to improve the international organization for peace. I think we can take leadership in the providing of example and advice for the improvement of material standards of living throughout the world. Above all, I think we can take the leadership in proclaiming the doctrines of liberty and justice and in impressing on the world that only through liberty and law and justice, and not through socialism or communism, can the world hope to obtain the standards which we have attained in the United States. Our leaders can at least stop apologizing for the American system, as they have been apologizing for the past fifteen years.

If we confine our activities to the field of moral leadership we shall be successful if our philosophy is sound and appeals to the people of the world. The trouble with those who advocate this policy is that they really do not confine themselves to moral leadership. They are inspired with the same kind of New Deal planned-control ideas abroad as recent Administrations have desired to enforce at home. In their hearts they want to force on these foreign peoples through the use of American money and even, perhaps, American arms the policies which moral leadership is able to advance only through the sound strength of its principles and the force of its persuasion. I do not think this moral leadership ideal justifies our engaging in any preventive war, or going to the defense of one country against another, or getting ourselves into a vulnerable fiscal and economic position at home which may invite war. I do not believe any policy which has behind it the threat of military force is justified as part of the basic foreign policy of the United States except to defend the liberty of our own people.

4

In order to justify a lend-lease policy or the Atlantic Pact program for mutual aid and for arming Europe in time of peace or the Marshall Plan or the Point Four program beyond a selective and limited extent, any such program must be related to the liberty of the United States. Our active partisanship in World War II was based on the theory that a Hitler victory would make Germany a serious threat to the liberty of the United States. I did not believe that Germany would be such a threat, particularly after Hitler brought Russia into the war, and that is the reason I opposed the war policy of the Administration from the elections of 1940 to the attack on the United States at Pearl Harbor in December 1941.[1] The more recent measures for Marshall Plan aid on a global scale—and to the extent of billions of dollars of American taxpayers' money—and the Atlantic Pact arms program are and must be based on the theory that Russia today presents a real threat to the security of the United States.

While I may differ on the extent of some of these measures, I agree that there is such a threat. This is due principally to the facts that air power has made distances so short and the atomic bomb has made air power so potentially effective that Russia today could do what Hitler never could do—inflict serious and perhaps crippling injury on our cities and on our industrial

[1] See Appendix.

plants and the other production resources which are so essential to our victory in war.

Furthermore, the Russians combine with great military and air power a fanatical devotion to communism not unlike that which inspired the Moslem invasion of Europe in the Middle Ages. The crusading spirit makes possible a fifth-column adjunct to military attack which adds tremendously to the power and danger of Russian aggression. The Russian threat has become so serious today that in defense of the liberty and peace of the people of the United States I think we are justified in extending economic aid and military aid to many countries, but only when it can be clearly shown in each case that such aid will be an effective means of combating Communist aggression. We have now felt it necessary in order to protect the liberty of the United States against an extraordinary special threat to adopt a policy which I do not believe should be considered as part of any permanent foreign policy. We have been forced into this not only because of the power of Soviet Russia but because the United Nations has shown that it is wholly ineffective under its present charter. The new temporary policy may be outlined as follows:

1. We have had to set up a much larger armed force than we have ever had to do before in time of peace, in order to meet the Communist threat. I believe this effort should be directed particularly toward a development of an all-powerful air force.

2. We have had to adopt as a temporary measure the policy of extending economic and military aid to all those countries which, with the use of such aid, can perhaps prevent the extension of Russian military power or Russian or Communist influence. We have backed that up by announcing definitely to Russia that if it undertakes aggression against certain countries whose independence is important to us it will find itself at war with us. This is a kind of Monroe Doctrine for Europe.

3. We have had to adopt a policy of military alliances to deter, at least, the spread of Communist power. To control sea

and air throughout the world, the British alliance is peculiarly important. Again, we hope that with the decline of Russian power and the re-establishment of an international organization for peace such alliances may be unnecessary.

I opposed that feature of the Atlantic Pact which looked toward a commitment of the United States to fight a land war on the continent of Europe and therefore opposed, except to a limited degree, the commitment of land troops to Europe. Except as we find it absolutely essential to our security, I do not believe we should depart from the principle of maintaining a free hand to fight a war which may be forced upon us, in such a manner and in such places as are best suited at the time to meet those conditions which are changing so rapidly in the modern world. Nothing is so dangerous as to commit the United States to a course which is beyond its capacity to perform with success.

In the course of later chapters I shall discuss the wisdom of this temporary policy and apply it to the particular situations which we face throughout the world. But it must always be considered, I believe, as a temporary expedient. It cannot avoid the possible danger of involving us in war with Soviet Russia, but it should not provoke a war which otherwise might not occur.

5

The main point of this preliminary statement, however, is to emphasize that our foreign policy must always keep in mind, as its ultimate goal, the peace and security of the people of the United States. Most of our Presidents have been imbued with a real determination to keep the country at peace. I feel that the last two Presidents have put all kinds of political and policy considerations ahead of their interest in liberty and peace. No foreign policy can be justified except a policy devoted without reservation or diversion to the protection of the liberty of the American people, with war only as the last resort and only to preserve that liberty.

2. The Place of the President and Congress in Foreign Policy

NO ONE can question the fact that the initiative in American foreign policy lies with the President. But, if I can judge from my mail and from many considered editorial expressions, the American people certainly do not believe or intend that his power shall be arbitrary and unrestrained. They want a voice in the more important features of that policy, particularly those relating to peace and war. They expect their Senators and Congressmen to be their voice. Before discussing the correctness of the principles of foreign policy, therefore, I shall try to define the place of Congress and the President under our Constitution. The debates in the Senate in early 1951 had even more to do with the question of who shall determine policy than with policy itself.

There can be no question that the executive departments have claimed more and more power over the field of foreign policy at the same time that the importance of foreign policy and its effect on every feature of American life has steadily increased. If the present trend continues it seems to me obvious that the President will become a complete dictator in the entire field of foreign policy and thereby acquire power to force upon Congress all kinds of domestic policies which must necessarily follow.

The fundamental issue in the "great debate" was, and is,

whether the President shall decide when the United States shall go to war or whether the people of the United States themselves shall make that decision. Also, for many years the State Department has been developing a theory that almost any action can be taken by executive agreement, which does not absolutely require any congressional approval at all, instead of by the treaty method prescribed in the Constitution. Undoubtedly, the necessity of obtaining a two-thirds vote in the Senate is very difficult and has encouraged many people to think that this development was necessary. But if the treaty method is not satisfactory, then the Constitution should be amended to provide for the approval of all executive agreements and to define the scope of and effect of such agreements much more clearly than at present.

More and more the State Department has assumed to do many things which are beyond its power in the field of trade, by an executive agreement known as the General Agreement on Tariff and Trade (GATT). It has insisted that the Executive have the power to raise and lower tariffs, through reciprocal trade agreements, within constantly widening limits and without the slightest shadow of a standard prescribed by law. Political agreements as important as those made at Yalta have never been submitted to Congress at all.

The execution of international agreements, such as the United Nations Charter and the Atlantic Pact, has now given rise to extended claims that the President can do anything which can be related to those treaties and anything recommended by the international commissions there created, without any consultation whatever with Congress.

I think it is fair to say that the State Department has adopted an attitude of hostility toward Congress and an unwillingness to submit any matter to Congress if it thinks it can possibly carry it through without such submission. It shows a complete distrust of the opinion of the people, unless carefully nursed by State Department propaganda.

The matter was brought to an issue by the intervention of

the President in the Korean War without even telling Congress what he was doing for several weeks. And it was brought still further to the fore by the proposal that we commit troops to an international army under the control of a council of twelve nations. I do not think that the American people have ever faced a more serious constitutional issue or one which in the end may present a greater threat to their freedom.

In the long run, the question which the country must decide involves vitally not only the freedom of the people of the United States but the peace of the people of the United States. More and more, as the world grows smaller, we are involved in problems of foreign policy. If in the great field of foreign policy the President has the arbitrary and unlimited powers he now claims, then there is an end to freedom in the United States not only in the foreign field but in the great realm of domestic activity which necessarily follows any foreign commitments. The area of freedom at home becomes very circumscribed indeed.

If the President has unlimited power to involve us in war, then I believe that the consensus of opinion is that war is more likely. History shows that when the people have the opportunity to speak they as a rule decide for peace if possible. It shows that arbitrary rulers are more inclined to favor war than are the people at any time. This question has become of tremendous importance, perhaps greater than any particular problem of troops to Europe or the manner in which the Korean War shall be conducted. The claims made by the President of the United States and by various documents presented to the Senate by the executive representatives far exceed the powers claimed by President Roosevelt during World War II, those claimed by President Truman when the United Nations Charter was passed, and those claimed by President Truman when the Atlantic Pact was adopted.

On January 4, last, President Truman, commenting on the Coudert resolution to bar him from sending more troops to Europe without the consent of Congress, said emphatically that he did not need the permission of Congress to take such action.

On January 11, at a press interview, according to the Washington *Post:*

"Mr. Truman, whose right to send troops to Europe recently was challenged by Senator Taft, said he had the power to send them any place in the world. This, he said, had been repeatedly recognized by Congress and the Supreme Court.

"A reporter asked Mr. Truman in effect what would happen if Congress tried to tie his hands by putting restrictions in the appropriation bills for the forces to be sent to Europe.

"That, said the President, was up to Congress. If they wanted to go to the country about it, he said, he would go with them—and he recalled that he licked them once."

At the President's conference a week later, on January 18, according to the press:

"He repeated that his constitutional authority to send American forces to Europe to take up their positions in an integrated European army was clear and did not depend upon the consent of Congress. What he would be glad to have, he said in substance, was a Senate expression that affirmed his constitutional authority."

Furthermore, a document was submitted to Congress, entitled *Powers of the President to Send the Armed Forces Outside the United States,* dated February 28, 1951, which was printed, though not endorsed, by the Joint Committees on Foreign Relations and Armed Services of the Senate. This document contains the most unbridled claims for the authority of the President that I have ever seen written in cold print. In effect, the document asserts that whenever in his opinion American foreign policy requires he may send troops to any point whatsoever in the world, no matter what the war in which the action may involve us. The document also claims that in sending armed forces to carry out a treaty the President does not require any statutory authority whatever, and it does not recognize the difference between a self-executing treaty and one which requires, even by its own terms, congressional authority. It ends with the most sweeping claims for power:

As this discussion of the respective powers of the President and the Congress in this field has made clear, constitutional doctrine has been largely molded by practical necessities. Use of the Congressional power to declare war, for example, has fallen into abeyance because wars are no longer declared in advance. The Constitutional power of the Commander in Chief has been exercised more often, because the need for armed international action has grown more acute. The long delays occasioned by the slowness of communications in the eighteenth century have given place to breathtaking rapidity in the tempo of history. Repelling aggression in Korea or Europe cannot wait upon Congressional debate. However, while the need for speed and the growth in the size and complexity of the armed forces have enlarged the area in which the powers of the Commander in Chief are to be wielded, the magnitude of present-day military operations and international policies requires a degree of Congressional support that was unnecessary in the days of the nineteenth century.

That seems a very gracious concession to Congress. Congress no longer has any power to act. It is simply given the right to support the President after the President has acted. I was shocked in the very beginning of this controversy by the speed with which blind partisans in the administration rushed to the defense of the proposition that the President can make war and warlike commitments. Senator Connally, the chairman of the Foreign Relations Committee, made this extraordinary assertion on the floor of the Senate:

The scope of the authority of the President as Commander in Chief to send the Armed Forces to any place required by the security interests of the United States has often been questioned, but never denied by authoritative opinion.

That certainly is a complete misrepresentation of the discussion of these constitutional powers which has taken place since the foundation of the nation.

As soon as I made my speech of January 5, 1951, the New York *Times* rushed to get Professor Henry Steele Commager to throw together in a day or two a superficial article, published in its Sunday magazine at that time, in which he asserts that the President has the right to start war whenever he sees fit to do so.

Editors of many newspapers and magazines accepted without question the State Department's claims, made without any basis, that history books have listed more than one hundred and thirty cases where United States Presidents sent United States armed troops into action "to defend the national interest."

The most interesting but alarming thing is that there seem to be so many responsible people in the country who follow the party line of the State Department in foreign policy with complete blindness as to where it may lead, in spite of the fact that it has led us a long way toward disaster recently and in spite of the fact that it may be the opposite of a policy adopted six months earlier. In so doing they blithely dismiss all interest in the maintenance of popular government under the Constitution. They are obviously afraid of popular government, thinking that the people are too dumb to understand foreign policy and might oppose policies which these blind followers favor but which the people think may lead to war.

Of course, the President has wide powers in foreign policy, but the framers of the Constitution provided expressly that only Congress could do certain things. Those powers are expressed in Section 8 of Article I. Of course, Congress is given the power, and the exclusive power—

To declare war, grant letters of marque and reprisal, and make rules concerning captures on land and water.

To raise and support armies, but no appropriation of money to that use shall be for a longer term than two years.

That reflects a certain and definite suspicion of a possible desire on the part of some President to set up a great permanent military force. Further powers of Congress as stated in Section 8:

To provide and maintain a navy.

To make rules for the government and regulation of the land and naval forces.

There are other powers, such as calling forth the militia and disciplining the militia.

The Constitution also provides that the President shall have the power to make treaties, but only by and with the advice and consent of the Senate, provided two thirds of the Senators present concur. The President's relationship to the armed forces is stated only in Section 2 of Article II of the Constitution:

The President shall be Commander in Chief of the Army and Navy of the United States . . .

There is one very definite limit—and I think it is admitted by every responsible authority who has discussed the problem —on the President's power to send troops abroad: he cannot send troops abroad if the sending of such troops amounts to the making of war. I think that has been frequently asserted; and whenever any broad statements have been made as to the President's power as Commander in Chief to send troops any-where in the world the point has been made that it is always subject to that particular condition.

Perhaps no one has been quoted more on this general sub-ject than has my father, who discussed this question in various lectures, articles, and books. My father had wide experience, as governor general of the Philippines, Secretary of War, and President of the United States. He never served in a legislative body, and, if anything, I think he leaned toward the power of the Executive. The clearest statement of the question, I believe, is contained in his article in the June 6, 1916, number of the *Yale Law Journal,* from which I quote:

When we come to the power of the President as Commander in Chief, it seems perfectly clear that Congress could not order battles to be fought on a certain plan, and could not direct parts of the Army to be moved from one part of the country to another. The power to declare war is given to Congress. . . . This is necessarily a limitation on the power of the President to order the Army and the Navy to commit an act of war. It was charged against President Polk that he had carried on a foreign war against Mexico before Congress had authorized it or declared it, and it is difficult to escape the conclusion that the act of President Wilson in seizing Veracruz was an act of war without congressional authority, at the time it was committed, though a resolution authorizing it was pending, and had passed one House and was passed in a very short time after the act by the other House, constituting a valid ratification.

It is not always easy to determine what is an act of war. The President has the authority to protect the lives of American citizens and their property with the Army and the Navy. This grows out of his control over our foreign relations and his duty to recognize as a binding law upon him the obligation of the Government to its own citizens. It might, however, be an act of war if committed in a country like England or Germany or France which would be unwilling to admit that it needed the assistance of another government to maintain its laws and protect foreign relations, but would insist that injuries of this sort must be remedied through diplomatic complaints and negotiations. . . . Of course, the President may so use the Army and Navy as to involve the country in actual war and force a declaration of war by Congress. *Such a use of the Army and Navy, however, is a usurpation of power on his part.* (Italics mine.)

Some may feel that if the President can do certain things there is no sense in arguing that he has no right to do them. But the division and limitation of powers is the very basis of our constitutional system, and decisions regarding the proper limits of such powers affect the validity of many other actions, such as the right of Congress to pass legislation to restrain the President's authority to send troops abroad in such a way as to involve the country in war. True, the President perhaps cannot be prevented from usurping power, but we can only presume the President will follow constitutional laws passed by the people's representatives.

Most of the cases which have been cited as authority for the President sending troops abroad are cases where the use of our troops was limited to the protection of American citizens or of American property.

The Boxer Rebellion is frequently cited; but in that case troops were sent into China because the legations in Peking were besieged and the legitimate Chinese Government was unable to defend them against the rebellious Boxers. So the various nations sent their troops there, in order to rescue those who were in the legations. That was a clear effort to protect American lives, to protect American diplomatic lives which were threatened contrary to the law of nations; and certainly it was not an act which would necessarily involve us in war.

The case of the Mexican rebellion is referred to, and it was referred to by my father, who said that President Polk's right was challenged. It was challenged by a very distinguished American, Abraham Lincoln, who on February 15, 1848, wrote his law partner with reference to Polk's use of the Army against Mexico:

Allow the President to invade a neighboring nation whenever he shall deem it necessary to repel an invasion, and you allow him to do so whenever he may choose to say he deems it necessary for such purpose, and you allow him to make war at pleasure. Study to see if you can fix any limit to his power in this respect. If today he should choose to say he thinks it necessary to invade Canada to prevent the British from invading us, how could you stop him? You may say to him "I see no probability of the British invading us," but he will say to you, "Be silent: I see it, if you don't."

Lincoln said further:

The provision of the Constitution giving the war-making power to Congress was dictated, as I understand it, by the following reasons: Kings had always been involving and impoverishing their people in wars, pretending generally, if not always, that the good of the people was the object. This our convention understood to be the most oppressive of all kingly oppressions, and they resolved to so frame the Constitution that no one man should hold the power of bringing this oppression upon us.

I do not believe history will defend as lawful the action of President Theodore Roosevelt in seizing Panama.

On the other hand, that action was certainly not the making of war.

The administration pamphlet to which I have referred cites the case of Iceland and says that none of the constitutional restrictions was regarded by President Roosevelt "as a limitation on his power to use the Navy in the North Atlantic Area or send troops to Iceland and Greenland and other places." My own view is that President Roosevelt clearly usurped authority when he sent American troops to Iceland to replace the British troops there in 1941, and I made a vigorous protest at the time on the floor of the Senate and was supported also by Senator Danaher. I quote from the speech which I made on July 10, 1941, and which, as far as I remember, was answered by no one except Senator Connally.

Mr. President, on Monday the President of the United States notified the Senate that forces of the United States Navy had already arrived in Iceland in order to supplement, and eventually to replace, the British forces now stationed there. This action was taken in accordance with an understanding reached by the President with the Prime Minister of Iceland, frankly inspired, however, according to the Prime Minister, by the British Minister to Iceland, who explained to him that British forces in Iceland were required elsewhere, and suggested that he apply to the United States for forces. The Prime Minister stressed the fact that the United States forces must be strong enough to meet every eventuality; and the President promised that the Government of the United States would immediately send troops, apparently including the United States Army as well as the Navy, to supplement, and eventually to replace, the British forces now there. Judging from the various press reports, it is likely that 80,000 American boys are in course of being sent to Iceland 2400 miles from any American territory, and substantially a part of the continent of Europe.

In my opinion, the President has no legal or constitutional right to send American troops to Iceland. It is not an agreeable task for me to question the authority of the President to take any action which he has taken in the name of the Government of the United States; but I believe it would be most unfortunate if the Senate of the United States should acquiesce without protest in acts of the President which might nullify for all time the constitutional authority distinctly reserved to Congress to declare war.

It would be a tremendous stretching of the Constitution to say that without authority from Congress the President of the United States can send hundreds of thousands of American soldiers to Europe when a war is raging over that entire Continent, and the presence of American troops would inevitably lead to war. The President cannot make aggressive war. Neither can he intervene in a war between two other nations, because such intervention, even though it does not immediately involve a physical attack on one of the combatants, is clearly the making of war.

There has been no attack on the United States and no threat of attack. The action of the President is not only beyond the powers which the Constitution has granted to him, but it is a deliberate violation of his pledge to the American people.

The speech which I made in the Senate on March 29, 1951, refers to various supporting statements by J. Reuben Clark, Assistant Secretary of State under the Hoover administration, by Quincy Wright, professor at the University of Chicago, and by Attorney General George E. Wickersham. We have perhaps even more eminent authority to the effect that the President has no right to send troops abroad in such a way as to intervene in a war between two nations. When the Germans broke through in France in June 1940 Mr. Roosevelt gave every encouragement to France and England to go on fighting. The end of his letter of June 15, 1940, to Premier Reynaud is enlightening, and I quote:

In these hours which are so heart-rending to the French people and yourself, I send you the assurances of my utmost sympathy, and I can further assure you that so long as the French people continue in defense of their liberty, which constitutes the cause of popular institutions throughout the world, so long will they rest assured that matériel and supplies will be sent to them from the United States in ever increasing quantities and kind.

I know that you will understand that these statements carry with them no implication of military commitments. Only the Congress can make such commitments.

Franklin D. Roosevelt

Yet Harry S. Truman in the case of Korea undertook to do exactly the thing which Franklin Roosevelt said he had no power to do.

In the case of Korea it was claimed that the intervention could take place under the United Nations Charter on the call of the Security Council. Of course the Security Council never acted under Articles 41 and 42 of the United Nations Charter, and even if it had done so the obligation to send troops is clearly limited by Article 43. That Article provides that troops can only be called for when an agreement has been entered into with the Security Council specifying the number and character of the assistance to be furnished. No such agreement has ever been entered into. The United Nations Participation Act of 1945, approved by President Truman, also made it clear that any agreement which required the providing of military aid must be subsequently approved by Congress, and, of course, it never has been. Not only that, but President Truman sent a cable from Potsdam when the United Nations Charter was under consideration, in which he said: "When any such agreement or agreements are negotiated, it will be my purpose to ask the Congress by appropriate legislation to approve them." The charter was adopted largely on that assurance, but now the President's claims are far beyond what they were then.

The State Department itself admits that the action of the Security Council in the Korean case was only a recommendation under Article 39. If the President can carry out every recommendation of the Security Council or the General Assembly supported by the vote of the American representative whom he can direct, then he has almost unlimited power to do anything in the world in the use of either troops or money. The Security Council might recommend that the nations should rebuild the canals on the Tigris and Euphrates and establish a vast Garden of Eden in the Kingdom of Iraq. According to the argument made, the President would then have power to use all American forces to establish such an economic project. On the same theory, he could send troops to Tibet to resist Communist aggression or to Indo-China or anywhere else in the world, without the slightest voice of Congress in the matter. If that could be the effect of an international treaty, we had better watch closely the approval of any such treaty in the future. Of course, it is not.

My conclusion, therefore, is that in the case of Korea, where a war was already under way, we had no right to send troops to a nation, with whom we had no treaty, to defend it against attack by another nation, no matter how unprincipled that aggression might be, unless the whole matter was submitted to Congress and a declaration of war or some other direct authority obtained.

The question of sending troops to Europe is certainly much more complicated. There is no doubt about the President's power to send troops to occupied Germany. There is no question that he can send them if he wants to do so, as Commander in Chief of the Army and Navy. Whether Congress could limit the number to be sent is a point which may be open to question. However, certainly the President has the power to do so if Congress does not act.

I think he can station troops in a friendly country if such

country asks that the troops be sent and if there is no imminence of attack and if they are stationed there for some possible convenience in repelling a general attack upon the United States itself.

Particularly, it seems to me that the President of the United States may station air forces and may send the Navy to odd places throughout the world, as Presidents have done many times, because the sending of such forces does not necessarily involve or threaten involvement in war. Such forces can be easily withdrawn in case an attack is made upon the country. There is no question about their remaining there and becoming involved in a war, if our country determines that it does not wish to become involved in a war.

But it seems clear to me that the sending of troops without authorization by Congress to a country under attack, as was done in Korea, is clearly prohibited. The sending of troops under the Atlantic Pact as a part of a defensive operation against Russia without previous authority from Congress appears to me to be also prohibited, because the fact that these countries are threatened by an actual attack is the very justification and reason for sending the troops. The only reason for sending troops is to defend a country against a threatened military attack which would necessarily involve the United States in war.

The European Army Project, however, goes further than merely sending troops to implement the Atlantic Pact. It involves the sending of troops to an international army similar to that which was contemplated under the United Nations Charter. It is an international army, apparently established by twelve nations, with a commander who is appointed by the twelve nations. It seems to me perfectly clear that the President's power as Commander in Chief does not extend to the delegation of that power to a commander who is chosen by any other nation or any other group of nations. I think it is perfectly clear that he cannot enter into an agreement of that kind to set up an international army without submitting the agreement to Congress.

The proponents of executive power have referred to many statements from the writings of Professor Edward S. Corwin of Princeton, a noted authority on constitutional law, but on this subject he says:

The outstanding fact about the Administration's proposal from the point of view of constitutional law is that it raises a question of first impression. The proposal is novel, unprecedented and consequently the precedents do not apply to it, except perhaps in the case of Iceland in 1941. The Administration's present proposal incurs the danger of precipitating war, and it raises vast questions regarding finance and the internal welfare of the country. Congress has the right to safeguard its war-declaring power, and it is duty bound to protect the domestic interests to which its other powers extend. In fact, the right of the President to merge American forces with an army, which he cannot exclusively command, seems very dubious. Congressional authorization under the necessary and proper clause would seem to be essential.

Throughout the 1951 debate the Administration tried to avoid this question of setting up an international army, but there can be no doubt that that was in fact the project, as I point out in Chapter Five.

Under that project the President actually appointed General Eisenhower, in a letter in which he stated:

The North Atlantic Treaty nations have agreed on the defense organization for Europe and at their request I have designated you as supreme allied commander, Europe. I view their request as a pledge that their support of your efforts will be complete and unequivocal.

When the President of the United States went that far he exceeded his authority. Up to that point, what was done at Brussels was a recommendation of the Council under the Atlantic Pact. When the President undertook to carry out that recommendation he usurped the powers of Congress. He had no authority to carry out that particular agreement made at Brussels, without submitting it to Congress.

Apparently the Administration is afraid that there was such an exceeding of authority, for it has represented the whole project now as merely the sending to Europe of a few divisions, which we can withdraw at any moment, but only to co-operate with the other nations in case war comes in a general defense under the terms of the Atlantic Pact.

But whether there is to be an American army or an international army, I do not believe the President has the power without congressional approval to send troops to one country to defend it against a possible or probable attack by another country.

Such action may perhaps be authorized by treaty, but it has not been authorized either by the United Nations Charter, as I have shown, or by the Atlantic Pact.

In my opinion, the Senate resolution and the concurrent resolution adopted by the Senate on April 4, 1951, was a clear statement by the Senate that it has the right to pass on any question of sending troops to Europe to implement the Atlantic Pact, that it is unconstitutional for the President to send any troops abroad to implement that pact without congressional approval, at least until war comes and Article 5 takes effect. It has been said that this resolution is not a law, and, of course, that is true, but the declaration can be implemented by the Appropriations Committee and by other legislation when legislation becomes appropriate. There can be no doubt that it is a legislative act and that it clearly asserts the power of Congress and the Senate.

No one can prevent the President continuing to assert his power as President, and it may be that he does have the ability to involve the United States in war, even when he has no right to do so; but I think a great forward step in defense of constitutional law has been taken by the definite position now asserted by the Senate.

The President acts at his own peril, if he chooses to usurp authority which the representatives of the people have asserted that he does not possess.

3. International Organization as a Means of Securing Peace with Liberty

ENTIRELY apart from any immediate threat of military aggression against the United States, I have always favored an international organization to promote the peace of the world and therefore of the United States. My father campaigned vigorously during World War I in behalf of a proposed League to Enforce Peace. President Wilson wrote a similar program into the Versailles Treaty in the form of the League of Nations, and I always favored strongly our joining that League. On August 26, 1943, before the American Bar Association, I urged the formation of a world-wide organization of sovereign nations, outlining the general character of that organization, and I quote from my speech:

The plan for an enforced peace which accords most closely with the ideals of the American Republic and of the Atlantic Charter, is that for an Association of Nations to include the United Nations and the Neutrals and, after a period of probation, the Axis nations. It would be supported by covenants between sovereign nations agreeing to determine their disputes by the law of nations and judicial decision, or by arbitration. It would further be supported by covenants to join in the use of force against any nation determined to be an aggressor by the decision of some international tribunal. Frankly, this is an obligation which the American people may be loath to undertake, but I believe they will undertake it, because they know that if war is not prevented at the start, under modern conditions it is more than likely to spread throughout the world.

But there are certain conditions to be insisted on.

First, force should not be called for against any nation because of any internal domestic policy, except rearmament in excess of a quota imposed or agreed to. Interference in domestic policies, even such vital matters as tariffs or the treatment of minorities, would be more likely to make war than prevent it. The test is: is the subject one on which the people of the United States would be willing to have other nations interfere with our internal actions? If not, we should not attempt to impose such interference on others.

Second, the covenant must be preceded by an economic arrangement fair to all nations, and by political arrangements providing for proper self-determination. The covenant, of course, must provide for the revision of boundaries and obligations, but essentially we will be asked to guarantee the status quo. We cannot make that guarantee unless the status quo is fair to all peoples and gives them a chance to live, and therefore affords a reasonable hope that peace can be maintained.

Third, I believe that any obligation to use force in Europe should only be secondary, not to be effective until the peace-loving nations of Europe have exhausted their own resources. This is in accord with Mr. Churchill's suggestion of a Council of Europe under the Association of Nations. We cannot help solve the problems of Europe unless the great majority of the European nations first agree on what that solution should be.

I supported the resolution by the Republican Conference at Mackinac Island, "favoring responsible participation by the United States in a postwar co-operative organization among sovereign nations to prevent military aggression, and to attain permanent peace with organized justice in a free world." This was the language of Senator Vandenberg, and it contains the soundest, most concise statement of the proper basis of international organization.

I supported the Connally resolution adopted by the Senate of the United States on November 5, 1943. I voted for and supported the United Nations Charter in the Senate on July 28, 1945.

I was never satisfied with the United Nations Charter and stated my criticism definitely at the time. The fundamental difficulty is that it is not based primarily on an underlying law and an administration of justice under that law. I believe that in the long run the only way to establish peace is to write a law, agreed to by each of the nations, to govern the relations of such nations with each other and to obtain the covenant of all such nations that they will abide by that law and by decisions made thereunder. I criticized the Connally resolution, because it omitted any reference whatever to the establishment of a rule of law. It is extraordinary that the original Dumbarton Oaks proposals for a United Nations Charter omitted all reference to justice. The final charter, largely through the work of Senator Vandenberg, does recognize the importance and desirability of justice, but it does so only in the most general way, and the Chapters dealing with the Security Council, which form the heart of all enforcement, require the Security Council to make such decisions as will "maintain peace and security," without any reference to justice.

It is true that Article 24 contains a general provision that in discharging its duties the Security Council shall act in accordance with the purposes and principles set forth in Chapter I; and it is also true that this chapter includes justice as one consideration. But the reference to justice and international law in paragraph 1 of Article 1 and the reference to justice in paragraph 3 of Article 2 seem to be related only to the settlement of disputes by peaceful means. If the Security Council has to make a definite decision looking to the employment of force, it is done primarily on the basis of maintaining peace and security.

Peace and security are not synonymous with justice. It might well be that the Security Council, acting in full compliance with the charter, could take property from one nation to which it justly belonged and give it to another, because it felt that would promote peace. So Mr. Chamberlain agreed to the transfer of Sudetenland to Germany. By substituting the maintenance of peace and security for law and justice we authorize the basing of decisions on expediency, and for expediency there are no rules which cannot be changed by the majority to fit its desires in a particular case.

It should also be pointed out that the veto power given to prevent the Security Council from making recommendations under Article 39 or from using sanctions and force under Articles 41 and 42 completely dispels the idea that any system of universal law is being established, for surely nothing can be law if five of the largest nations can automatically exempt themselves from its application.

It is suggested that the charter can be made satisfactory by eliminating the veto power. I do not see how we ourselves can agree to eliminate our veto power, if decisions of the Security Council to use force are based on expediency rather than law. It seems to me that peace in this world is impossible unless nations agree on a definite law to govern their relations with each other and also agree that, without any veto power, they will submit their disputes to adjudication and abide by the decision of an impartial tribunal. The agreement to abide even by unfavorable decisions was the essence of the arbitration treaties which my father, when President, negotiated with England and with France. It was unfortunate that they were defeated by the Senate. Until nations are willing to enter into such an agreement, international progress toward peace is bound to fail.

Such progress is probably dependent even more on building up in the world public opinion in behalf of law and justice between nations. No matter what the covenants made, an aggressor who violates his covenants can only be suppressed if a real world public opinion unites against him, in enthusiastic military support of those who fight for peace and justice. There is no such world public opinion today, and so we find the attempt to punish aggression in Korea at best a stalemate and the attempt to punish aggression by Chinese Communists a complete failure.

I have thought that our State Department has lost complete touch with the principles of liberty and justice on which this nation was founded. Certainly those who drafted the Dumbarton Oaks proposals could not have been enthusiastic supporters of American principles. My opposition to the Nuremberg trials was based on the fact that those trials violated every instinct of justice which I have grown up to regard as fundamental.[1] Even more, by trying to clothe a matter of policy in the robes of justice, they discredited for many years the ideals of justice between nations.

We see also in the matter of our trade relations with other nations a demand by the State Department for unlimited power under the Reciprocal Trade Agreement Act and a complete unwillingness to be bound by law or standards of any kind. The brazen disregard of law in the Korean enterprise and in the setting up of an international army in Europe is further evidence that our State Department has long since repudiated any serious respect for law and justice. It is now dominated far more by the philosophy of the economic planner who feels that the Government must decree the life of its citizens and of the world on a strictly opportunistic and expedient policy. My own feeling is that this policy in the field of foreign affairs, unless restrained, can only lead to arbitrary and totalitarian government at home, as foreign affairs comes more and more to dominate our domestic activities, and to war in the world.

The net result of the terms of the charter has been to destroy the usefulness of the United Nations as far as the prevention of

[1]See Address of Robert A. Taft at Kenyon College, October 5, 1946, on "Equal Justice under Law."

aggression is concerned. I pointed this out in my speech on the charter in 1945, when I said:

All the discussion about force is of minor importance because it can never be used to solve any major crisis. If the charter had been in effect, Japan would have vetoed any action against itself on the invasion of Manchuria and of China. Italy would have vetoed any action against itself on the invasion of Ethiopia. In some ways the organization would have been less effective even than the League of Nations. The charter could not use force if Russia were to invade Poland or seize the Dardanelles from Turkey. Even attacks by satellite nations of one of the great powers might be engaged in safely if a great power had agreed in advance to exercise the veto power. If one of the five great powers violates the charter, and vetoes action against its own violation, the charter is for all practical purposes dissolved in failure.

When the North Koreans attacked on June 25, 1950, it happened that Russia was boycotting the Security Council, and the resolution calling for action against the North Korean aggression was therefore passed without dissent.

On June 28, 1950, I questioned the legality of the United Nations' action, because Article 27 of the charter clearly provides that decisions of the Security Council on all matters shall be made by an affirmative vote of seven members, including the concurring votes of the permanent members. There was no concurring vote by Russia, but we overrode this objection without considering how it might be raised against us in the future. Furthermore, we took this action without considering the fact that if the Chinese Communists attacked and the Russian representative returned to the Security Council the United Nations could not follow up its action against the Korean Communists by similar action against Chinese Communists.

If the Russians had planned it that way, they could not have done better. Did they perhaps arrange the North Korean attack when they were boycotting the United Nations, so that the United Nations might take an abortive action? Did they deliberately ignore the point I have just made, relating to affirmative votes, knowing that they could later block action against China? In any event, the President committed the United States to the Korean War as an undertaking of the United Nations, deluded as to a power which never has existed under the charter. His moral position was unassailable, but he did not realize the implications of what he started.

We have tried to bypass the limitations on the power of the Security Council by asking for action by the General Assembly when a veto has been exercised in the Council. Under the charter this body has never been intended to have any power to call on governments for action or do more than recommend. It would be most unwise for us to build up such power in the General Assembly. No nation has contracted to abide by any decision of the General Assembly. There is no obligation to comply with its recommendations. Furthermore, we would only have one vote among sixty, which sometime in the future, even in the very near future, may subject us to very arbitrary treatment.

Certainly this did not excuse the long delay of the Assembly in denouncing the Chinese Communists as aggressors. Its whole dilatory action repudiates the very basic theory of the charter that the United Nations is formed to prevent aggression and maintain peace. But action taken by the Assembly today can only have moral effect.

Those who are blaming the United Nations should much more blame the limitations of the charter and our own Government for forcing United Nations' action beyond its permanent power to perform.

I believe we ought to formulate the amendments which would create an ideal organization. But for the present we can only make use of the United Nations, as best we may, as a diplomatic weapon, and through it we may hope for more general support of our position against Communist aggression. Perhaps it may assist in establishing more friendly relations with Russia. But as far as military policy is concerned I see no choice except to develop our own military policy and our own policy of alliances, without substantial regard to the non-existent power of the United Nations to prevent aggression. The very adoption of the Atlantic Pact seems to me to constitute recognition of the impotence of the United Nations.

At this point I might discuss the other alternative form of international organization which is being urged strenuously upon the people of the United States, namely, a world state with an international legislature to make the laws and an international executive to direct the army of the organization.

The theory of an international state, bearing the same relation to nations and their citizens as our federal Government bears to the states and their citizens, appears to me, at least in this century, to be fantastic, dangerous, and impractical. It is proposed that it have a supreme legislature, executive, and court. It would maintain an all-powerful military force able to dominate all nations. It would control all trade, all seaports, and all airports within the various nations. Such a state, in my opinion, would fall to pieces in ten years.

The whole idea is based on the union of the thirteen colonies in 1787. But those colonies were made up of men of similar origin, similar methods of thought, similar ideals, with similar forms of government. They lived approximately the same kind of life, with similar standards of living. Even in that case one single difference resulted in a violent civil war about seventy-five years later which almost destroyed the Union. Here we would be attempting to unite peoples who do not understand even how their new fellow citizens begin to think; we would join democracies with dictatorships, Moslem states with Christian states, the Brahmin with the Rotarian, men who talk only Japanese with men who talk only English. We would attempt to unite the most highly civilized with the aborigines, the workman who earns twenty dollars a day with the coolie who earns twenty cents a day. The difficulties of holding together such a Tower of Babel under one direct government would be insuperable.

Furthermore, if it could remain in existence at all, it would not remain democratic—if a state including dictatorships like those of Russia, Communist China, Argentina, and Yugoslavia could ever have been democratic. True freedom depends on local self-government, effective access of the people to their individual rights. Sometimes I question whether the United States has not reached the limit of size under which the people of a nation can have a real voice in its government. Certainly a world government at Geneva or Panama would listen more closely to the voice of well-organized pressure groups than to the voice of an ordinary American citizen from city, small town, or farm.

It is significant that the British Empire, because of its size, has moved toward decentralization of government and has to-day no over-all legislative body, no over-all executive, and no over-all police force. If Canada and Australia and New Zealand and South Africa and Eire are regarded as too diverse to be consolidated into one government, what about China, Japan, India, Russia, Switzerland, and Ethiopia?

But above all, anyone who suggests such a plan is proposing an end to that liberty which has produced in this country the greatest happiness, the greatest production, the highest standard of living the world has ever seen. He is proposing to tear up the American Constitution which has made this nation the greatest power for good in the world, setting an example of successful popular rule to the entire world. We are asked to scrap a tried plan, which up to this time has successfully maintained our liberty at home and abroad and afforded to this country the protection against invasion which is the alleged purpose of all international plans. It would subject the American people to the government of a majority who do not understand what American principles are and have little sympathy with them.

Most people who think carelessly of a world state seem to think that it would be run by the United States. But we, of course, would have a very minor voice in the character of legislation. We would be the natural target of all other nations for taxation and all kinds of economic discrimination. The controversies which would arise in trying to pass legislation would almost certainly produce hundreds of disputes which could easily lead to war between constituent states, for civil war is as possible as any other war. Most such disputes would never arise at all under a covenant between nations admitted to be sovereign in their own territory. The plan would promote war instead of preventing it.

I cannot conceive of a responsible American statesman willing to subject the great principles we have developed in this country to destruction by an alien majority. A world state might bring peace for the moment, but it would be the peace of dictatorship and in a few years would plunge us again into world-wide war. Any international organization which is worth the paper it is written on must be based on retaining the sovereignty of all states. Peace must be sought not be destroying and consolidating nations but by developing a rule of law in the relations between nations.

There are two steps which might be taken to improve the United Nations. We might press for a convention to write amendments to the charter. That would probably be blocked by Russia. We might set up an organization of nations within the United Nations under a more ideal charter. There was an opportunity to do this in the case of the Atlantic Pact, but the State Department chose to negotiate a military alliance. If all the Atlantic Pact nations agreed to a new form of international organization based on law and justice without veto, it could operate between themselves and settle all disputes among them. An example of success might lead to the new organization's becoming the real power within the façade of the United Nations.

4. The Russian Menace. How It Was Created

I POINTED out in 1945 that the defects of the United Nations Charter make it completely useless against the aggression of one of the five permanent members. This result has been made apparent sooner than might have been expected by two facts—first, the revelation that Russian Communism has a spirit of aggression which recognizes no laws or obligations (as we were told by all those who knew anything about it), and, second, an Administration policy which deliberately built Russia up to a position of dangerous power. These developments have created a menace from Soviet Russia, which has brought the weakness of the United Nations Charter into sharp focus and made it apparent that the charter cannot possibly deal with the aggression of one of the five permanent members. It has forced upon the United States the necessity of adopting what we hope are temporary policies to insure our own safety, rather than a complete reliance on the international organization.

Even during the war the policies which were adopted by the United States completely ignored the possibilities which might occur after the war had been won. The exclusive interest of the Administration was to bring the fighting to an immediate close, no matter what might be the ultimate outcome of the peace. Hanson Baldwin, in his book *Great Mistakes of the War*,[1] points out clearly that the whole policy of unconditional surrender was an invitation to unconditional resistance, that it discouraged opposition to Hitler, lengthened the war, and left a vacuum in Germany into which only Russia could move. He points out the stupidity of our fear that Russia might make a separate peace with Germany and the equally stupid assumption that we had to invite Russia into the Japanese War, when in fact we had already won that war. These curious misconceptions led us throughout the war to an almost suppliant attitude toward Russia. We acted as if it were a favor to us for Russia to accept our lend-lease assistance. We accepted Russia's military demands and overruled every British objection to policies which were bound to make Russia stronger after the war.

The concessions made at Teheran, Yalta, and Potsdam and our later policies in the Far East were such as to build up Soviet Russia to a position of power which today does indeed present a threat to the security of the United States. The reasons for our giving Russia everything that it requested—and even more—are complex, but perhaps some of them are now apparent. After the Teheran conference (November 28–December 1, 1943), in an address which I made on June 8, 1944, I pointed out the danger to ultimate peace from the negotiations at that time. I said:

The danger to the accomplishment of an association of nations to preserve the peace does not come today from so-called isolationists or any unwillingness on the part of our people to go ahead. It comes from the current policy of Mr. Stalin and the failure of this country to have any definite foreign policy at all.

The most revealing picture of the minds of Roosevelt, Churchill, and Stalin was contained in the two articles by Forrest Davis in the *Saturday Evening Post*. The material was evidently obtained directly from the President. According to those articles, the President's foreign policy up to this time, his "great design," is "to secure the goodwill of Russia as a sincere and willing col-

[1]New York, Harper & Brothers, 1950.

laborator in postwar settlements." To accomplish this purpose
he concentrated on personal charm and avoided all issues which
might bring about a difference of opinion. He seems prepared to
sacrifice all principles of foreign policy to appease Russia. He
"avoided the slightest cause of offense to the Kremlin" and
avoided any statement of fundamental principles, such as Wilson
insisted on in World War I. He feared to renew our offer of good
offices in the Russo-Polish controversy. He promptly came to the
support of the Communist Tito in Yugoslavia. He made an immediate and generous response to Stalin's demand for a share in
the surrendered Italian fleet, or its equivalent. Its equivalent is
now said to include one of our own cruisers. He urges the Finns
to quit the war at once without reference to Soviet terms. He
"quipped and yarned, relieving tension," suggesting compromises
between Churchill and Stalin. No agreement was reached at
Teheran on the disposition of a defeated Germany "or in truth on
any other major postwar issue." Yet on most of these issues Mr.
Stalin stated his own policy "pushing his claims, directly and indirectly, in the vast areas of Europe which he has staked out as his
sphere of influence." Stalin had a hearing on his point of view regarding Poland and expressed his view that since the British had
not done so well in managing the Balkans, Russia should have a
whirl at it. When the three leaders got around to the Baltic States,
Stalin upheld his contention as to the legality of the Soviet-con-
trolled plebiscites in Estonia, Latvia, and Lithuania, so the President thought there was little point in pressing his own principles
that a plebiscite be held under impartial auspices, because the subject was "touchy with reference to Russia."

The week before these articles appeared I stated in Cleveland
that I had every hope the Russians would agree to conditions on
which permanent peace might be founded but that Mr. Roosevelt did nothing whatever at Teheran even to suggest restraint
to Mr. Stalin. I did not imagine, however, that Stalin had reaffirmed so many Russian policies without serious dissent. A man
like Stalin certainly assumes that silence gives consent.

From these Davis articles it is clear that our policy is based on
the delightful theory that Mr. Stalin in the end will turn out to
have an angelic nature and do of his own accord those things

which we should have insisted upon at the beginning before supplying $4,000,000,000 worth of lend-lease supplies.

Forrest Davis's articles do not contain any clear statement of Mr. Churchill's attitude, but from his public statements it is reasonably certain that he intends to urge at every point the interests of the British Empire. In his speech of May 24 [1944] he discussed the promised organization of nations and spoke of a "world-controlling council . . . comprising the greatest states which emerge victorious from this war." As an afterthought he says that there must also be a world assembly of powers, whose relations to the world executive or controlling power he is in no position to define. No doubt Mr. Roosevelt also listened to this conception of a league of nations bossed by England, Russia, and America, without expressing any dissent that might produce a conflict of opinion. . . .

I do not wish to judge finally any of the problems I have discussed, but I do want to suggest that they are far more important and far more difficult than the theoretical discussion of the terms of a covenant of an association of nations; and their solution along present lines would make the association a mere shell.

At Yalta (February 4–11, 1945) Mr. Roosevelt was a sick man, but the general policies which he followed at Teheran were also followed at Yalta.

They were supplemented by something perhaps rather more sinister in the indirect influence of communism and Communists on American statesmen. It is interesting to note that in the book published by Edward R. Stettinius, Jr., he makes it clear that, while he went to Yalta as Secretary of State, he had nothing to say about the negotiations on the important and unfortunate Agreement Regarding Japan, which has had such disastrous results. He was told that W. Averell Harriman, who was then ambassador to Russia, had all the necessary data and that he would look after most of these negotiations. According to Stettinius, Harry Hopkins, as well as Averell Harriman, assisted the President in his discussions on the Far East and the Agreement Regarding Japan. It is significant that Alger Hiss was also at the conference and evidently made his influence felt as one of three State Department experts who traveled with Stettinius to Yalta.[2]

Mr. Hopkins and Mr. Harriman apparently accepted completely the idea that Russia was a peace-loving nation, for it is so designated in the joint Declaration on Liberated Europe agreed to at Yalta. At Teheran Roosevelt signed a declaration welcoming all nations into a "world family of Democratic Nations," of which Russia was apparently already one in the eyes of Roosevelt, Hopkins, and Harriman.

Our first ambassador to the Soviet Union, William C. Bullitt, in an article in *Life* (August 30, 1948), made the following statement:

> The Department of State employed its influence with Washington correspondents and columnists to add rosy colors to the Soviet picture. . . .

> The President and Hopkins gradually began to be swept away by the waves of propaganda they had started. In spite of the President's statement of February 10, 1940: "The Soviet Union is run by a dictatorship as absolute as any other dictatorship in the world," they developed the theory that the Soviet Union was a "peace-loving democracy" and bestowed favors on persons who subscribed to this perversion of the truth. Able and patriotic officers of the Department of State and the Foreign Service who knew the truth about the Soviet Union and refused to lie in favor of the Communist dictatorship were moved to unimportant posts. Clever young men who knew the truth but cared more about their careers than their country and were ready to testify that "Stalin had changed" were promoted rapidly—and became contemptible profiteers of American disaster.

Henry Wallace, former Vice-President and at the time of Yalta Secretary of Commerce, had made speeches about the "new democracy," to be built by the people of the United States and of Russia. He said that anyone suggesting that the

[2]Edward R. Stettinius, Jr., *Roosevelt and the Russians* (Garden City, N.Y., Doubleday & Company, 1949).

aims and purposes of the two peoples were irreconcilable was criminal, that in some ways Russia was more democratic than America.[3] Joseph E. Davies, American ambassador to Russia before Harriman, expressed the view that the Soviet leaders were "sincerely devoted to peace" and that what they most desired was to live as good neighbors in a world at peace.[4] Hopkins said it was ridiculous to think of Stalin as a Communist. He was a Russian nationalist.[5] In any event, all these men were led into a complete misconception of the real purposes of the Russian Government and its communist character.

My own view is that the Communists in our Government, in the labor unions, and among the writing fraternity in both New York and Hollywood were concerned with influencing people who were in a position to affect public opinion or public policy or others who could influence such people. They planted exactly the philosophy which was adopted—that communism was probably not the form of government for the United States but that it was, in fact, a form of government more or less consistent with American ideals.

I could never understand how any man who went through even an American high school could reach such a conclusion. Communism, from my point of view, denies every principle of Americanism. It denies liberty. Certainly in Soviet Russia there is no one who can be safe from spying and seizure by the Soviet police. Certainly there is none of its boasted equality, for the members of the Party have most of the privileges and they are only a small proportion of the total population. Certainly there is no justice. The Soviet simply uses the courts as instruments of public policy. They do not even admit the possibility of an impartial tribunal in any matter in which communism is in any way concerned. Every man is either for them or against them. Communism denies religion. It denies God Himself. It is hard

[3]Speeches, May 24, November 8, 1942.
[4]Prologue to film, *Mission to Moscow,* 1943.
[5]John T. Flynn, *The Roosevelt Myth* (New York, Devin-Adair Co., 1948), pp. 340–341.

to find any philosophy which is more the antithesis of American principles, and yet many of our policy makers at Teheran and Yalta seem to have accepted the professions of the Communist leaders as to their interest in liberty, peace, and equality.

The result was that at Yalta our policy makers accepted all Stalin's promises that he would set up a free Poland, for instance, and free states in the Balkans, although he had never kept a promise which he had made. They accepted these promises without any means of enforcing them. Stalin and Hitler together had really started World War II, and Stalin had joined in the partition of Poland by moving into Poland from the east, just as Hitler moved in from the west.

The influence of the military mission under General Marshall has not been made so clear, but apparently it was responsible, at least indirectly, for the many concessions made to Russia in the Far East, by insisting on the necessity of Russia entering the war against Japan. Admiral Leahy alone felt it was unnecessary.[6] General Marshall must at that time have over-estimated the strength of Japan and deliberately ignored the Japanese peace overtures.[7]

In any event, the net result of the negotiations was to permit Russia to enter Berlin first and to set her up in a Russian zone, which occupies a dominating position in Germany today. The lines of that zone were so drawn as to give the Russians the most dominating military positions in Germany and bring them within eighty miles of the Rhine at Mainz and within a hundred miles of the Ruhr. We did not even reserve a right-of-way to get into our own zone in Berlin, a mistake which cost us many hundreds of millions of dollars and many lives in maintaining the air lift. We seem to have conceded the influence of Russia in Czechoslovakia and, of course, in eastern Austria.

[6]William D. Leahy, *I Was There* (New York, Whittlesey House, 1950), p. 293.

[7]See particularly Ellis M. Zacharias, *Behind Closed Doors* (New York, G. P. Putnam's Sons, 1950), p. 55 *et seq.*

In short, we established Russia in the dominating positions of Central Europe, at Berlin, at Prague, and at Vienna, from which they dominate Central Europe, cut off Eastern Europe, and threaten the security of Western Europe and, therefore, that of the United States itself.

It does not appear that these concessions were necessary. Our troops could have reached Berlin before the Russians if they had not been called back. We withdrew from Dresden and Leipzig, which we had already occupied. General Patton would have been in Prague the next day, but he was called back so that Czechoslovakia could surrender to Russian generals, and his own book shows that he was not pleased with that recall.[8]

In matters of reparation the Russians got all the best of it, and for many years after that time industrial plants were being shipped from Germany into Russia to be used to build up the military strength of Soviet Russia. At the same time we adopted, in effect, the Morgenthau Plan, which consistently reduced the productive strength of Germany and carried out even more effectively the general theory of the war of unconditional surrender, a policy which removed the possibility of Germany's being restored as a state strong enough to resist Russian aggression.

In the Far East our action seems to be even less understandable. We agreed to Russia's taking over the same position in Manchuria which Japan had occupied, in effect a military control of Manchuria.[9] This was contrary to every principle of American foreign policy since the day of John Hay and the open door in China. We actually had gone to war with Japan because of its aggression in Manchuria and in other parts of China, and yet, having defeated Japan, we agreed to Russia's moving in toward the dismemberment of China. We turned

[8]George S. Patton, Jr., *War as I Knew It* (Boston, Houghton Mifflin, 1947), p. 327.

[9]The provisions of the Agreement Regarding Japan were as follows:

The leaders of the three Great Powers—the Soviet Union, the United States of America and Great Britain—have agreed that in two or three

over southern Sakhalin and the Kuril Islands without strings of any kind, although the many islands which we had captured in the Pacific are to be held under a trusteeship from the United Nations. Russia today has occupied islands down to within a very short distance of northern Japan, so that it presents a real threat to Japan in case a war occurs, and it might be almost impossible to defend the northern part of the Japanese archipelago.

This whole agreement was made without even letting Chiang Kai-shek know for four months that we had bargained away his most important industrial province.[10] Chiang was an ally who had fought by our side for five years and stood out against Japanese attack and Japanese cajolery during all that

------

months after Germany has surrendered and the war in Europe has terminated the Soviet Union shall enter into the war against Japan on the side of the Allies on condition that:

1. The status quo in Outer Mongolia (The Mongolian People's Republic) shall be preserved;

2. The former rights of Russia violated by the treacherous attack of Japan in 1904 shall be restored, viz:

(a) the southern part of Sakhalin as well as all the islands adjacent to it shall be returned to the Soviet Union,

(b) the commercial port of Dairen shall be internationalized, the pre-eminent interests of the Soviet Union in this port being safeguarded and the lease of Port Arthur as a naval base of the USSR restored,

(c) the Chinese-Eastern Railroad and the South-Manchurian Railroad which provides an outlet to Dairen shall be jointly operated by the establishment of a joint Soviet-Chinese Company, it being understood that the pre-eminent interests of the Soviet Union shall be safeguarded and that China shall retain full sovereignty in Manchuria;

3. The Kuril Islands shall be handed over to the Soviet Union.

It is understood, that the agreement concerning Outer Mongolia and the ports and railroads referred to above will require concurrence of Generalissimo Chiang Kai-shek, The President will take measures in order to obtain this concurrence on advice from Marshal Stalin.

The Heads of the three Great Powers have agreed that these claims of the Soviet Union shall be unquestionably fulfilled after Japan has been defeated.

For its part the Soviet Union expresses its readiness to conclude with the National Government of China a pact of friendship and alliance between the USSR and China in order to render assistance to China with its armed forces for the purpose of liberating China from the Japanese yoke.

Joseph V. Stalin/Franklin D. Roosevelt/Winston S. Churchill
February 11, 1945

[10]He was not informed until June 15, 1945. Department of State Publication 3573, *United States Relations with China* (1949), p. 116.

period, and yet, in effect, we abandoned him to the demands of Soviet Russia. This action put the Russians in a position in Manchuria where they could furnish arms and assistance to the Chinese Communists, which, of course, they promptly did. For some time General Wedemeyer attempted to assist the Nationalist Government in taking over control of Manchuria, but it was blocked by the Russian occupation of Port Arthur, Dairen, and Russia's control of the railroads.[11] Then the State Department went further. It certainly expressed every sympathy with the Chinese Communists and did everything it could to discredit the Nationalist Government of Chiang Kai-shek. That government probably was corrupt in many ways, as charged, but certainly corruption has been a feature of every Chinese Government for centuries, and we do not seem to be entirely free of it in the United States itself.

The Far Eastern Division of the State Department was inspired, to say the least, by strong prejudice in favor of Chinese Communists,[12] and that seems to have been shared also by Secretary Acheson himself. General Marshall was sent to China to insist that Chiang Kai-shek take Communists into his cabinet,[13] and he did his best to force that result. Chiang refused to do so. His refusal certainly seems to have been justified by what happened in Czechoslovakia when Communists infiltrated the cabinet there. Yet, when Chiang did refuse, Marshall cut off further military aid to Nationalist China, from August 1946 until May 1947. We held up definite promises which had been made to Nationalist China, while the Russians threw everything into the assistance of the Chinese Communists. General Wedemeyer's appointment as

[11]This is clearly described by Hu Shih, former Chinese ambassador to the United States, writing in *Foreign Affairs,* October 1950.

[12]Among others, Patrick J. Hurley, ambassador to China, set this forth in his letter of resignation to President Truman dated November 26, 1945. Department of State, *op. cit. supra,* p. 582.

[13]In his press conference of December 18, 1946, President Truman was asked, "Are we urging the Nationalist government in China to accept Communists in the Cabinet?" "It has been our policy all along," Truman replied. Washington *Post,* December 19, 1946.

ambassador to China was canceled by Mr. Acheson because the Chinese Communists objected.

At the Potsdam Conference (July 17–August 2, 1945) for the first time, apparently, some suspicions about Soviet good faith began to arise in the minds of those who were running American foreign policy, particularly Secretary Byrnes, but, nevertheless, at Potsdam, President Truman reaffirmed all the agreements made at Yalta and approved the Morgenthau policy in Germany and even went beyond the Yalta agreement in some of the workings out of that agreement.[14] His agreements finally sealed the fate of the Baltic peoples, of Poland, of Czechoslovakia, and of the Balkan states.

From that time on our policy of conceding everything in Europe to Russia was gradually changed, I believe very largely under the influence of Senator Vandenberg, who, at San Francisco, saw how completely impossible it was to deal with the Russians. Working with Vandenberg, Secretary Byrnes finally refused to go along with any plan which would give Russia a predominating position throughout Germany. He threatened to resign unless Henry Wallace was dismissed from the Cabinet, and President Truman complied with his advice. Gradually, in Europe our whole position changed, and we took a definite position against the expansion of Russian influence in any degree. We adopted the Marshall Plan, which proposed to give assistance to countries threatened by Russian infiltration and by communism from within. We adopted a policy of giving military aid to Turkey and Greece, which were under direct threat of attack by the Communists. We finally ratified the Atlantic Pact and agreed to go to war with Russia if it attacked any member of that pact. In short, we completely reversed our policy in Europe and adopted the general policy of checking the advance of communism in every way in which it could possibly be checked.

[14]See Sumner Welles, *Seven Decisions That Shaped History* (New York, Harper & Brothers, 1951), pp. 205, 206.

On the other hand, in the Far East we continued to encourage the growth of the power of communism.

In spite of the recommendations of the Wedemeyer report on China, we finally abandoned Chiang Kai-shek. The Administration fought efforts to provide money for arms to Chiang and refused to carry out the policy along that line decreed by Congress. Even when Chiang Kai-shek had retired to Formosa the Administration refused to give him any assistance whatever. On January 5, 1950, the President said: "The United States Government will not provide military aid or advice even to Chinese forces on Formosa."

I said in an interview in December 1949 that I supposed our policy of checking the growth of communism would, of course, apply to the defense of Formosa. Here was an island which could be easily defended with sea and air power, containing eight million people who certainly were not friendly to communism and occupying a very strategic position in the Far East. I was sneered at both by the President and Secretary Acheson. I found that the State Department had already issued an instruction to our representatives in the Far East, saying that "Formosa has no special military significance" and that it was strictly a Chinese affair. I quote from the State Department instruction:

Loss of the island is widely anticipated and the manner in which civil and military conditions there have deteriorated under the Nationalists adds weight to the expectation. . . .

In areas of insistent demand for United States action, particularly in the United States itself, we [the members of the State Department] should occasionally make clear that seeking United States bases on Formosa, sending in troops, supplying arms, dispatching naval units or taking any similar action would (a) accomplish no material good for China or its Nationalist regime; (b) involve the United States in a long-term venture, producing at best a new area of bristling stalemate and at worst possible involvement in open warfare.

Mr. Acheson in his testimony at the MacArthur hearings claimed that our policy had always been to keep the Communists out of Formosa by every means except the use of American armed forces. Why we should have hesitated to use the American Navy, in view of our infinitely more dangerous and expensive venture into Korea six months later, it is difficult to see. Mr. Acheson claims that the memorandum deliberately misrepresented our real policy, for the purpose of saving our face if Formosa fell, as he believed it would. In other words, either we were lying then or the State Department is lying now.

In view of the President's refusal to give even advice to Chiang and in view of the terms of the memorandum of December 23, 1949, it is impossible to believe Mr. Acheson or escape the conclusion that the State Department wanted to see Formosa taken over by the Communists.

Mr. Acheson indicated further that America might recognize Communist China. There is no doubt that the attitude of the Administration toward Formosa and its general weak position toward the spread of communism encouraged the war in Korea.

In January 1950 Secretary Acheson stated clearly that we would fight if Japan, Okinawa, or the Philippines were attacked, but we could give no guarantee beyond that point. We had withdrawn our troops from Korea, and we thus made it clear that we would not defend South Korea if attacked.

Furthermore, we even failed to arm South Korea. We had declared when we withdrew our troops that we would give armed assistance to Korea. The Mutual Defense Assistance Act of 1949 authorized the President "to furnish military assistance to the Republic of Korea," and $10,500,000 was set aside to carry out the provisions of the authorization, but none of it was ever used. And, although Assistant Secretary Webb testified specifically, before both the House and the Senate, that the appropriation was sought for the purpose of helping Koreans to deter external aggression, the Administration policy was changed to provide only small arms for internal security.

The President himself in June 1950 finally admitted that the Government forces in Korea were armed only "to prevent border raids and to preserve internal security." In other words, the South Koreans had no tanks, no heavy artillery, and no planes to resist the Russian-equipped forces of North Korea.

This action was taken in complete disregard of General Wedemeyer's report of September 9, 1947, so long suppressed by the Administration. He had pointed out that the "North Korean People's Communist Army of approximately 125,000 is vastly superior to the United States-organized Constabulary of 16,000 Koreans equipped with Japanese small arms. . . . The creation of an American controlled and officered Korean Scout Force, sufficient in strength to cope with the threat from the North, is required to prevent the forcible establishment of a Communist government after the United States and Soviet Union withdraw their occupation forces."

There is no doubt that the Administration's weak policy invited the Communist attack. The Communists took the Secretary of State at his word. They knew that we had permitted the taking over of China by the Communists and saw no reason why we should seriously object to the taking over of Korea. The Korean war and the problems which arise from it are the final result of the continuous sympathy toward communism which inspired American policy. The result today is that Chinese Communists have taken over practically all of continental China, and from that point they have sent armies into Korea and Tibet, and are threatening Indo-China, Burma, Thailand, and all of Southeast Asia.

The result of the Administration policy, therefore, has been to build up the strength of Soviet Russia, so that it is, in fact, a threat to the security of the United States. Our liberty is threatened by the Russian military strength, backed up by the fifth-column strength which the Russians are always able to develop among Communists in every nation in the world.

I feel that Russia is far more a threat to the security of the United States than Hitler in Germany ever was. There are several reasons for that belief. Principally, it is based on the great development of air power, which permits airplanes to be built that can fly from Russian territory or Russian bases all the way to the United States. It is certainly possible that Russian planes can be built, in time, able to fly to the United States and return. The Russians also apparently possess the atomic bomb, or at least we have to allow for that in our plans. That means that while they attack other portions of the world they can also attack the United States, possibly destroy our cities, possibly destroy many of our key industrial plants, which are necessary for the conduct of war.

In any all-out world war we need a year or more to develop the production and the training which is necessary for all-out war and which can never be developed before war actually occurs. Therefore, the Russian air power does present a threat to our ability to do what we did in World Wars I and II. Furthermore, we cannot estimate the strength of Russian sabotage and fifth-column destruction. Soviet Russia is far stronger in that regard than Germany was at any time.

Of course, the Russians have much greater manpower than ourselves, and if they can also swing the manpower of China, as they seem to be doing at the present moment, they have an overwhelming superiority in manpower, if it can ever be brought to bear against the United States itself. I don't see how that can be done unless our air force is inferior and finally destroyed by the Russian air strength. Nevertheless, it is a feature of the situation which did not exist in the case of Germany.

Therefore, today we find ourselves with the greatest military threat from foreign sources we have faced since the days of the American Revolution. We find that the United Nations is a weak reed to lean upon, and we are forced, therefore, to the development of some other policy to combat Russian aggression.

Before the Korean War began the Administration had proceeded on the theory that the Russians and their satellite countries would not engage in military attack. This threat of Russian aggression existed before Korea, just as much as after Korea, but we had developed no consistent plan to meet it. The country was assured that the Army, Navy, and Air Force of the United States, which then cost approximately twelve to thirteen billion dollars a year, was adequate for the defense of the United States against any possible Russian aggression. That seemed a large sum to me, and I took the word of the Joint Chiefs of Staff.

It was in March 1950 that General Bradley, chairman of the Joint Chiefs of Staff, testified before the Senate Committee on Appropriations that he was satisfied that a budget of $13,000,-000,000 for fiscal year 1951, with about a million and a half men in uniform, was sufficient for the interests of the country. He evidently would have preferred some additional sum but stated that he did not recommend any such addition at that time, saying: "We do not have any way of knowing whether this figure should be $13,000,000,000, $14,000,000,000, or $15,000,000,000. We think we must not spend this country into economic collapse and spoil our industrial potential." He testified: "The Joint Chiefs of Staff never went along with this great big figure of $20,000,000,000." He said that if he came and recommended a $30,000,000,000 budget for defense he would be doing a disservice and that "maybe you should get a new chairman of the Joint Chiefs of Staff."

Of course the Korean War has occurred since that time, but the present program of forty to sixty billion dollars a year is not to meet the Korean War but to meet the powerful threat of Soviet Russia. The Korean War itself only takes one tenth of the total of men now requested and perhaps costs five or six billion dollars a year to conduct. The threat from Russia was exactly the same and from the same Russia in early 1950 as it is today. It is our policy which has changed.

Finally, on June 25, 1950, the North Korean Communists, inspired by Soviet Russia and armed by Soviet Russia, attacked South Korea. The President reversed the entire policy promulgated by the State Department up to that time and ordered American troops into Korea, first without and then with the approval of the United Nations. The Communist attack made it clear to the American people that the Russians would not stop at military aggression by the troops of their satellites and raised a presumption that they might not even stop at military aggression in the case of Russian troops themselves. The use of satellite troops for aggression is no proof that Russia will start a world war, but, in any event, we had to reconsider our entire position and determine what policies should be adopted to meet the Russian threat.

5. The Russian Menace. How Do We Meet It Throughout the World?

HOWEVER the Russian menace was created, we face now the problem of the best methods of meeting it and protecting the safety of the American people. If possible, we wish to find the policies which will deter Russia from military aggression and at the same time will not be so provocative themselves as to give Russia a sound reason for such aggression. We must adopt also policies which, if war unfortunately comes, will best defend America and enable us to achieve ultimate victory. But we must be always alert to explore every possibility of permanent peace and all changes in public opinion in Russia or the satellite countries which look in that direction.

There is much more agreement on the general character of the strategy to be adopted than is generally supposed. The violent differences that have arisen relate to the relative emphasis on the various tactical policies involved in that strategy and to the manner in which they have been and should be worked out. Generally speaking, we must strengthen the forces opposed to communism and combat to the extent of our ability the spread of communism, both in political power and in the minds of men. For the present our policy may be said to be one of containment, but it certainly carries the hope that we can

develop an affirmative policy which will constantly extend the
doctrine and the power of liberty.

The Administration seems to have accepted this strategy in
theory, since the days of Secretary Byrnes. I believe that Arthur
Vandenberg had most to do with reversing the policies of
Teheran, Yalta, and Potsdam, which I have described in
Chapter Four. He stiffened the attitude of Secretary Stettinius
at San Francisco. He counseled against concessions to Russia
in Europe which might have led to a Communist Germany.
He and Byrnes forced President Truman to eliminate the pro-
Communist Henry Wallace from his Cabinet. Senator Vandenberg was never consulted about the Far East, and the
change-over in policy there was not made. Senator Vandenberg said in the Senate on March 18, 1947:

This bipartisan foreign policy has been confined within rela-
tively narrow limits. It has applied to the United Nations. It has
applied to peace treaties in Europe. It has applied to nothing else.
I have had nothing to do, for example, with China policies or
Pan-American policies except within the United Nations, and at
times I have been satisfied with neither. The first I ever heard
of the Greco-Turkish policy was when the President disclosed his
thoughts ten days ago at the White House.

On April 16, 1947, Senator Vandenberg said in the Senate:
"I have been highly critical of the State Department's policy
heretofore in China, because it has looked toward the creation
of a coalition with Communists, and in my opinion no Communist ever entered a coalition for any purpose except to destroy it."

But today the Administration seems to admit the general
application of the anti-Communist strategy, whether prepared
to apply it everywhere or not. My basic criticism of Administration policy today is that no one seems to have worked out
a comprehensive plan for the application of this strategy or
any co-ordinated use of the many policies necessary to carry it
out. Have we any program, positive or negative, ready for use
in Yugoslavia or Iran or Burma or Indo-China? Furthermore,

no one seems to have recognized that there are serious limits to our economic and manpower capacity and that we must be selective and restrained in determining the extent to which we carry out our basic strategy. No one has given the people a long-term plan—for production, for spending and taxation, and for controls—or explained to the people in clear language the reasons and justification for the sacrifices which must be asked for.

The methods suggested to carry out the basic strategy may be summarized as follows:

1. The creation of powerful American armed forces.

2. Economic aid to countries where such aid will enable anti-Communist countries to resist the growth of communism from within.

3. Arms aid to countries where such aid will enable anti-Communist governments to resist aggression from without or armed Communist forces within.

4. Warnings to Soviet Russia or its satellites that armed aggression beyond certain lines or against certain countries will be regarded by the United States as a cause for our going to war.

5. The sending of American troops to a country threatened by attack from Russia or its satellites (European army) or where the attack has already occurred (Korea).

6. An ideological war against communism in the minds of men.

7. An underground war of infiltration in Iron Curtain countries.

ECONOMIC AND MANPOWER LIMITATIONS
FORCE THE UNITED STATES TO SELECT
AMONG THE MANY PROJECTS PROPOSED
TO CHECK COMMUNISM.

We must realize that there are definite economic and manpower limitations on American strategy.

The people of the United States constitute only 6 per cent of the population of the globe. Our raw materials are certainly not more than a third of the world's resources. Our huge production is still less than one third of the world's production. Our people cannot, and do not desire to, boss the internal affairs of other countries. They cannot send armies to block a Communist advance in every far corner of the world. Consequently, we must consider the cost of the policies we adopt, both in men and money, and we are forced to be selective in determining the relative value and cost of each project.

Of the seven policies I have listed above by far the most costly under present conditions is the first, the creation of American armed forces sufficient to meet any threat of attack on land, sea, and air. President Truman's 1952 budget called for the expenditure of forty billion dollars for our armed forces, compared to eight and one-half billion for all kinds of aid to foreign countries. While the building up of our own forces is the first and best method of providing security for our people, it is also, therefore, in its extreme form the most disruptive to our national life, our freedom, our progress, and even our production.

The exact size of the program is a question on which men may well differ, but it is not solely a military problem. For some years the Administration assured us that armed forces of approximately one and a half million men, costing about thirteen billion dollars, were sufficient to meet any threat. The Joint Chiefs of Staff joined substantially in this view, as I pointed out in Chapter Three. On July 1, 1951, although there seemed to be no agreed plan, it was suggested that we need three million five hundred thousand men in uniform, at a cost which may run from forty to sixty billion dollars a year, or more than four times the annual amount suggested before the Korean War. Yet that war only accounts for about one tenth of what is requested, and the Russian menace is about the same as it was on January 1, 1950.

On July 23, 1951, however, the President suggested in his

economic report that 3,500,000 men was only an interim goal, and that plans were being made for a substantially larger expenditure. Secretary Acheson sent word to the Foreign Relations Committee that twenty-five billion dollars for three years of foreign aid was a serious underestimate. This indicated a Federal budget of at least a hundred billion dollars a year for fiscal 1953 and fiscal 1954.

If we were engaged in all-out war, we would probably have to spend something like one hundred and fifty billion dollars a year to conduct that war. That would be half our present national output, and in World War II we spent about half of the output at that time. Undoubtedly, if we ask the military men today to propose projects which would give us supposedly absolute and one hundred per cent security against every possible contingency they would have us spend one hundred and fifty billion dollars today in time of peace, and they could present projects costing that sum. But we are not at war, and the condition we face may go on for five, ten, and even twenty years, according to some of the generals.

The truth is that no nation can be constantly prepared to undertake a full-scale war at any moment and still hope to maintain any of the other purposes in which people are interested and for which nations are founded.

In the first place, it requires a complete surrender of liberty and the turning over to the central government of power to control in detail the lives of the people and all of their activities. While in time of war people are willing to surrender those liberties in order to protect the ultimate liberty of the entire country, they do so on the theory that it is a limited surrender and one which they hope will soon be over, perhaps within a few months, certainly within a few years. But an indefinite surrender of liberty such as would be required by an all-out war program in time of peace might mean the final and complete destruction of those liberties which it is the very purpose of the preparation to protect.

Furthermore, the destruction of that liberty in the long run will put an end to the constant progress which has characterized this country during its 160 years of life, a progress due more than anything else to the freedom of men to think their own thoughts, live their own lives, and run their own affairs. It would require a complete surrender of all of our material and humanitarian aims to increase the standard of living of our people and of the people of our allies. All of those standards of living would have to be reduced, because even the most optimistic do not feel that we can have all the guns we want and all the butter we want at the same time.

It would be impossible to conduct any such all-out program without inflation. In World War II, in spite of complete controls, we saw an increase in prices, apparently permanent, of about 70 per cent, a depreciation of the dollar to sixty cents. I doubt if any government spending program calling for half the national income could be undertaken which would not involve an increase in prices of at least 10 per cent every year and a corresponding depreciation in the value of the dollar. This would mean the destruction of savings and life insurance policies. It would mean a constant race between prices and wages. It would mean hardship for millions, and doubt and uncertainty for many millions more. It would mean constant domestic turmoil and disagreement.

Finally, it would interfere with the very production which is the great basis of the strength of the United States and to which not only our own people but all of our allies look for ultimate victory if there should be a war with Russia.

The truth is, also, that the most foresighted person could not set up a preparation that would protect us against every conceivable contingency. One or two Pearl Harbors might lay us open to a dangerous attack. We have to choose those measures which will give us the most complete protection within our reasonable economic capacity. In short, there is a definite limit to what a government can spend in time of peace and still maintain a free economy, without inflation and with at least some elements of progress in standards of living and in education, welfare, housing, health, and other activities in which the people are vitally interested.

The question which we have to determine, and which apparently nobody in the Administration has really thought through, is the point at which we reach the economic limitation in time of peace on government expenditures and a military program. After that we must choose between the various measures contributing to our defense, to determine which are of first importance and which can be ignored without serious danger.

The number of men in uniform is the most convenient guide to the total cost of the program, although, of course, there are many other elements. Just after the Korean War the Chiefs of Staff wanted 2,100,000 men. In December 1950 they raised their sights to 2,700,000 men. Within thirty days after that they finally came in with the suggestion of approximately 3,500,000 men in uniform. Now a larger number is suggested.

At the time of writing the President's expenditure budget for fiscal 1952 is still approximately seventy billion dollars, including about forty-one billion dollars for the armed forces, plus six and one quarter billion dollars for arms to foreign countries. But, from various indications, this is not going to be the actual ultimate cost of the program now submitted. It is said that 3,500,000 men under arms will cost about ten thousand dollars per man for current maintenance and replacement of equipment, clothing and the like. This would be about thirty-five billion dollars a year, but apparently for a period of several years, while we are providing the heavier equipment such as heavy artillery, airplanes, and tanks, there would be an additional bill of from fifteen to thirty billion dollars so that the total cost of the armed forces may well be sixty-five billion dollars. If no cut is made in other domestic and foreign aid expenditures the total expenditure will be close to eighty-five billion dollars a year. It is anticipated now that the expenditure budget for fiscal 1953 will be eighty-nine billion and this does not include the further expansion suggested by the Presi-

dent in his Economic Report. Taxes, including those enacted
in 1950, are now estimated to yield sixty billion dollars, so that
it would take from twenty-five to forty billion dollars of additional taxes in order to balance the budget.

If to eighty-nine billion dollars we add about eighteen billion dollars for state and local taxes our total tax bill will be
one hundred and seven billion dollars, or approximately one
third of the gross national production. My own view is that
this is more than we can possibly stand without inflation. It
would be about 40 per cent of the national income; and 40
per cent of expenditure and taxes in Great Britain has destroyed private initiative and is socializing the country.

I fully agree with President Truman that we should balance
the budget, because one thing is certain: if we do not do so
we are bound to have substantial inflation, with all its dis-
rupting results. But we have to balance it by holding down
expenses as well as by increasing taxes.

For there is also a limit to the taxes that can be levied on any
uniform basis, without creating injustice and hardship and
inflation. If taxes are raised too high they are themselves
inflationary, even though the budget is balanced. When the
hardship of taxes is too great people succeed in one way or
another in passing them on into the price of the goods, which
is ultimately paid for by the consumer. The rise of prices in
this manner will be met in part, at least, by increased wages,
and those again increase costs and prices.

Theoretically, you can fix prices and wages and prevent any
such increase, but in practice, even in wartime, we have seen
that this cannot prevent some inflation, and in time of peace
it will be infinitely more difficult to enforce controls of this
kind. People are willing to make sacrifices for a temporary
period while their boys are fighting at the front, but we saw
after World War II that the moment that threat is over people
are no longer willing to submit to any general control. Black
markets sprang up immediately after the war. Corn was sold
for any price that could be obtained for it. All the legitimate

lumber yards were empty, and lumber was carted directly from the mills to the job and sold for any price that could be obtained. At one time 80 per cent of the beef was in the black market, and most of it was entirely beyond the control of the Price Administration at that time. The weakness of peacetime controls is likely to permit a much more rapid inflation than in time of war.

There is another limit to be considered—the number of men who can be drafted into the Army and taken out of productive life. Probably we can maintain our production, even though three and one half million men are employed in the armed forces, although I already hear complaints from many farmers who have relied on sons from eighteen to twenty-one to run their farms, to the effect that they will no longer be able to undertake the program of increased agricultural production on their farms. Any program of putting six million men into the Army certainly would develop a shortage of men in industry itself, at the very time that we are trying to increase industrial production for our allies as well as for ourselves. Reliable estimates have been made by experts on manpower available for the armed forces, which show that we cannot keep more than three and a half million men in the armed forces without increasing the regular term of service to more than the current two-year term. Such service is already a serious interference with the education of our boys, and the greatest limitation on individual freedom in peacetime the people have ever had imposed on them. Three years' universal service would be still more disruptive and obnoxious to the American people.

One of our main functions in the present situation is to increase the already great production necessary to give the raw materials and the support to the countries of the Atlantic Pact and to other countries throughout the world. We must not weaken ourselves by rampant inflation or shortage of manpower or destroy the morale necessary to keep our people productive even beyond the present figures.

In short, even though the United States has the greatest

production in the world, there is a definite limit to what we can do. We cannot and should not proceed on the theory that war will begin tomorrow. All-out mobilization can only be undertaken when war is certain.

WE SHOULD STRIVE TO LIMIT FEDERAL EX-PENDITURES DURING THE EMERGENCY TO ABOUT 75 BILLION DOLLARS

It is hard to set any exact figure beyond which the federal budget should not go. Marriner Eccles, in an article in *Fortune* magazine, November 1950, estimated that seventy-five billion dollars is a possible federal tax. Roswell Magill, writing in the *Saturday Evening Post* of August 1951, also indicates his belief that we cannot tax more than 75 billion a year without inflation. Any general increase in prices might justify a higher tax burden in dollars. My own view is that in President Truman's estimate of Federal expenses in fiscal year 1952 of seventy-one billion dollars we have almost reached the limit which the Federal government in peacetime should undertake to expend in a singe year, unless the emergency is so great as to justify a deliberate policy of inflation and loss of liberty.

Of course, expenditures can be reduced in several different ways. In the first place, they may be reduced by drastic cuts in non-defense expenditures. I should estimate that five billion dollars could have been taken out of the budget in this respect if you include the cut in various foreign aid programs. In a speech on January 5, 1951, I suggested that 3,000,000 men in uniform should be about the limit and that perhaps a study of military practices would show that we could get the same results with 3,000,000 men in uniform as are now sought with 3,500,000 men. To a layman there always seems to be a great waste of manpower in the armed services. Is it necessary, for instance, to employ 50,000 men in uniform and 20,000 civilians in order to put a division of 18,000 men in the front line? Could we not get the twenty-four divisions which seem to be the goal of the general staff for a land army, without putting 1,500,000 men into uniform for that purpose?

If I am even approximately right, the more enthusiastic proposals for 100 divisions of land forces in time of peace would wreck the country's economy and, in time, its morale. They would require 5,000,000 men in the land Army which would add 3,500,000 men to the proposals of the chiefs of staff, costing about thirty-five billion dollars more than the present program. I think it would be impossible to raise taxes to provide this amount of money, and that means more debt and certain inflation. We must be reasonable and selective in determining the military projects which we are going to undertake to meet the Russian threat.

THE EMPHASIS IN SELECTING MILITARY PROJECTS SHOULD BE ON AIR POWER

In selecting the projects upon which we expend the resources of the United States to the limit of our economic and manpower capacity we have to consider the whole military policy, in preparation for a possible attack by Russia on ourselves or on our allies. I have yet to see anyone who has been able to describe clearly just what a third world war would be like. One thing seems to be certain: it would not be like World War I or II. Air forces and the atomic bomb would play a greater part than ever before, but no one can measure exactly what their strength would be. Certain principles, however, appear to be fairly clear.

Our first consideration must be the defense of America. Whatever one may feel about the action of the United States in other parts of the world, no matter how much of an internationalist a man may be, one must recognize that this country is the citadel of the free world. The defense of the United States itself is, of course, the first goal of our own people, essential to protect our liberty; but it is just as important to the rest of the world that this country be not destroyed, for its destruction would mean an end to liberty everywhere and to the hope of restoring liberty where it has been lost. It seems obvious that the immediate problem of defending this country depends upon control of the sea and control of the air.

There is no question that we have the largest Navy in the world and, certainly, as long as the British are our allies complete control of the sea throughout the world, except as it may be hampered by Russian submarines or airplanes. We have a powerful Air Force, but it seems vitally necessary that that Air Force be increased until we have control of the air over this country and over the oceans which surround our continent. It should be capable of expansion in time of war, to secure as great air control as possible over the rest of the world and over the enemy country. With our resources and with Great Britain as an ally, that is not impossible. By the end of the last war we had practically complete control of the air over Germany and Japan, and it was the decisive factor in the completion of victory. Not only is the Air Force necessary for defense of America, but it is the one weapon that can damage the enemy bases, from which air attacks upon us can be made.

Whether war can be ended by air power alone may be open to question, but certainly sea and air power can achieve a complete protection while other forces are being developed to meet whatever goals may seem to be desirable in a third world war. Of course, an army of reasonable size is absolutely essential. We must have it for the defense of the American continent and our island possessions. A land army is necessary for the defense of air bases, further defense of islands near the continental shores, and for such occasional extensions of action into Europe, Asia, or Africa as promise success in selected areas. But it need not be anything like as large an army as would be necessary to begin tomorrow a land war on the continent of Europe or the continent of Asia.

The fact that the Air Force has deteriorated is due solely to the shortsightedness of this Administration and the Pentagon policy, which, in substance, refused any increase in Air

Force unless corresponding increases occurred in the Army and Navy. The Eightieth Congress in 1947 set up a congressional Aviation Policy Board. This Board reported to the Congress on March 4, 1948, recommending a seventy-group Air Force as a prerequisite for national security. A Citizens Advisory Commission set up by the President under Thomas K. Finletter also recommended a seventy-group Air Force. The Eightieth Congress in the supplemental defense appropriation bill of 1948 provided for such a force, and the Air Force increased from fifty-five groups in June 1948 to fifty-nine groups in December 1948. On December 31, 1948, however, a presidential directive required the Air Force to be cut to forty-eight groups. In 1949 the Eighty-first Congress provided for a buildup of the Air Force to fifty-eight groups again, ten more than recommended by the President, but the President, when he signed the fiscal 1950 Military Appropriation Act, directed the Secretary of Defense to place in reserve the amounts provided by the Congress for increasing the structure of the Air Force. The amount impounded by direction of the President totaled $775,450,000.

On October 5, 1949, I wrote:

The possession of the bomb by Russia emphasizes above everything else the necessity of building up an all-powerful air force. The only possible defense is a complete control of the air. If there is ever a third world war, it will be won by the nation who can most completely dominate the air. We should build up our own Air Force again to seventy groups. We must constantly improve our Air Force and our air defense.

But until the Korean War the President still insisted on holding the Air Force to forty-eight groups. The power of the land generals was sufficient to hold down the Air Force unless the budget could provide a corresponding increase in land forces. Now the increase is to be balanced by an even larger increase in the land forces. The 1952 budget proposes to spend twelve and one half billion dollars for the Air Force, eleven billion for the Navy, and fifteen and one half billion for the land Army.

Not only is an all-powerful air force the best possible defense for the United States, but it is also the best deterrent to war. Winston Churchill has said that the American possession of the atomic bomb and the possibility of its being used in an attack on Russia have been the principal deterrents to Russian aggression. It seems to me this must be true. The Russians are not going to be deterred by land armies until such armies are built up to a strong defensive force completely able to throw back armies of Russia and its satellites, and they can always attack before that point is reached. Certainly they have not been deterred by land armies in Europe from 1946 to 1951, because there have been no land armies there to deter them. They know that the destruction of their principal communications, bases, and industrial developments by atomic bombs may make it infinitely more difficult for them to succeed in any war. Every consideration, therefore, of American defense and also of the insurance of peace depends upon the development of an air force more efficient and more effective than the world has ever seen.

A superiority in air and sea forces throughout the world can achieve other purposes than mere defense. It can protect all island countries, Africa and South America. It can furnish effective assistance to all those nations which desire to maintain their freedom on the continent. It can achieve a balance of power under which more peaceful relations throughout the world can constantly be developed.

While defense of this country is our first consideration, I do not agree with those who think we can completely abandon the rest of the world and rely solely upon the defense of this continent. In fact, the very thesis of an effective control of sea and air by the free nations requires that we do interest ourselves in Europe and the Near East and North Africa and the Far East, so that Communist influence may not extend to areas from which it is still possible to exclude it by many methods other than land armies.

It seems to me that our battle against communism is in fact a world-wide battle and must be fought on the world stage. What I object to is undertaking to fight that battle, in the first instance, primarily on the vast land areas of the continent of Europe or the continent of Asia, where we are at the greatest possible disadvantage in a war with Russia. The first principle of military strategy is not to fight on the enemy's chosen battle-ground, where he has his greatest strength. We could not have a better lesson than has been taught us in Korea. A small war against a minor Russian satellite like North Korea has cost us tens of thousands of casualties and taxed the resources of our armed forces to the limit. Yet there we have had the advantage of a comparatively narrow peninsula, with both flanks protected by the sea, and of complete domination of the air. We cannot be sure that we can ever transport enough men and equipment to overcome the vast manpower supplied by the teeming millions of Russia and of China on the main part of the continent. Where there is complete disregard for human life, even the best weapons and equipment may fail to overcome a tremendous disadvantage in manpower.

Our position is not greatly unlike that of Great Britain, which dominated much of the world for a period of about two hundred years and brought about the balanced peace of the last half of the nineteenth century. The British had control of the seas and met every challenge to that control. There was no question of air power. They seldom committed any considerable number of British land troops to continental warfare, and when they did do so they were by no means successful. Marlborough fought very largely with mercenary troops and the troops of his allies. Napoleon was finally defeated by a combination of many nations, which did not contain more than twenty per cent of British troops. Yet control of the seas enabled the British in many places to develop power on the land, as in India. They supported one group of such countries against others and gave strong support to their friends in every country. They established garrisons at strategic points where sea power could protect them. It was the sea power of Britain which gave Britain a powerful influence on the continent of Europe itself.

It seems to me that by reasonable alliance with Britain, Australia, and Canada the control of sea and air can establish a power which never can be challenged by Russia and which can to a great extent protect Europe, as it has been protected now for five years through fear of what sea and air power can accomplish against Russia. There is no need for a specific line of defense in every section of the world, but we can exercise a power for peace over a vast area. If the Russians realize that our power in the final outcome of war cannot be challenged except on the continent of Eurasia, and perhaps not there in the final issue, and that it can do real damage to their own nation with the atomic bomb and otherwise, their purpose of military aggression in Eurasia itself may well wither. If they are convinced that they cannot achieve world conquest by military means they are likely to turn to their old love of propaganda and infiltration. Gradually, peaceful relations in Europe may grow again, for the desire of human beings for peace and comfort and normal human relations is a powerful force which will constantly assert itself.

I do not believe that our sea and air power should be used for aggressive purposes, but I do believe it should be available to assist those nations which ask for assistance to defend themselves against Communist aggression, to the extent that such power can be successfully and effectively used. In the first place, we should be willing to assist with our own sea and air forces any island nations which desire our help. Among those islands are Japan, Formosa, the Philippines, Indonesia, Australia, and New Zealand; on the Atlantic side, Great Britain, of course.

There is some question as to the ability of sea and air power to defend islands in reasonably close proximity to the coast, as are Formosa and Japan. Sea power there is seriously limited by submarines and mines, but we should make every possible effort to establish the ability of our Navy and Air Force to prevent any landing across salt water. The submarine problem must be solved at all costs.

The power of great sea and air forces is not necessarily limited to island nations. The policy I suggest certainly does not abandon to Communist conquest the continental nations. In the first place, we give economic assistance to many such nations, providing they want that assistance and use it effectively against communism. We give arms, as we are bound to do under the Atlantic Pact and as we are now doing in Indo-China, in Greece, in Turkey, in Formosa. An adequate modern air force should be able to bomb the communications of any aggressor, its army and air bases, and its manufacturing plants and thus not only deter aggression but seriously interfere with its success. Probably strategic air power cannot prevent a land advance, but it can certainly play a powerful part in the defense against such an advance and in the ultimate outcome of the war.

The commitment of a substantial American land army to continental soil is a much more serious problem. Broadly speaking, it is far less practical. Its expense is capable of indefinite expansion, once we are involved, as we have seen even in the Korean War. It is fighting the enemy on his chosen ground. As a general policy, I do not believe that in time of peace we should commit American troops to continental soil, or in time of war unless we are reasonably certain of success through the efforts of our own Army and our allies. I shall discuss later the special exceptions that apply because of developments in Europe and Korea.

But there are other examples in the world where it may even be wise or expedient to commit some land troops with a reasonable chance of success. The entire continent of Africa is connected with Asia, and certainly we might have to assist in defending the Suez Canal, as a means of maintaining our connections by sea and of defending Africa, where there are many strategic materials, valuable air bases, and a threat to South America. It may be possible to assist Spain. I should suppose that Singapore and the Malay peninsula could be defended by land troops if sea and air power is available on both sides of the peninsula. The extension of such aid by land troops, however, is a dangerous experiment, as we found in Korea. I doubt that, on principle, we should enter into any definite commitments in advance in time of peace, or undertake the job at all, unless we are sure it is well within our capacity and almost certain of success.

6. The Russian Menace. How Do We Meet It in Europe?

I BELIEVE that the general principles I have stated apply to Europe as well as to the rest of the world, but undoubtedly the special problems of Europe and its importance to the cause of freedom throughout the world force us to act there more vigorously and make some exceptions to the general rules of policy. Our cultural background springs from Europe, and many of our basic principles of liberty and justice were derived from European nations. American language and ideas, American institutions, and American methods of thought are largely derived from Europe. Our principles of government and our institutions are certainly more like those of Europe than like those of any other parts of the world. We recognize a common interest in promoting the prosperity of the entire world, through increasing our interchange of products, by encouraging trade and commerce. The overwhelming majority of the American people have the kindliest feelings for the people of Western Europe and certainly desire our relations to remain on the most friendly basis.

It is also true that outside of the United States the greatest productive ability of the world is centered in Europe, and the industrial capacity of Western Europe if added unimpaired to Russian capacity would make Russia a more dangerous threat to the United States than it is today. To some extent this argument may be overdone. Let us look at the actual situation which would exist in case of war. These European nations have asked us to go to war against Russia if Russia attacks them. We have agreed to do so. That means that if Russia does attack there will be a full-scale war, and it is likely that that war will be fought to the end. During that war the industrial potential of Western Europe can hardly be organized in time to be of great military value to the Russians. Industrial plants would be destroyed by bombing. The whole economy of these countries would be completely upset, as it was in World War II. The ability of Russia to restore European industry when it has once been disorganized cannot compare with our ability, and yet it took four years after the war and billions of our dollars to restore Europe to its industrial potential.

There is one other point that I would like to bring out. We speak of Western Europe as if it were a single country. It is nothing of the kind, and the efforts to make it such have completely failed up to this time. I believe that an alliance with England and a defense of the British Isles are far more important than an alliance with any continental nation and offer a much greater hope of success. With a British alliance there can be little doubt of our complete control of sea and air throughout the world. The British may be hard to get on with and we may have many differences with them, but I believe that both of us are determined to reconcile those differences.

The problem of Italy is almost entirely separable from that of the rest of Europe. Italy can only be defended as a separate project, and some modification of the Italian Treaty is required if there is to be any defense of Italy at all.

Germany, of course, is in a special situation. The Russian zone already extends far across Germany, at one point to within eighty miles of the Rhine. The best military opinion considers the defense of Germany impossible short of the Rhine, which would put most of Germany again under Russian control. Naturally enough, the Germans are not much interested in establishing an army, if war could only lead to their being another battleground between the powerful nations.

France is the only other large country, and its problems again are almost completely individual. Certainly France cannot be defended by us unless it shows a great interest in a strong army of its own.

It has been American policy to try to unify Western Europe, economically and politically, but that policy certainly has not been successful up to this time, and I am afraid it is contrary to human nature and geography. There is nothing even resembling a customs union, and only a slight relaxation of trade restrictions. The Benelux Union, which was supposed to set an example, has never become effective, because of the inability of reconciling the economic condition of Holland with that of Belgium. The Schuman Plan is encouraging, but Great Britain, the most important industrial nation in Western Europe, has refused to join.

I do not mean to suggest that we should give up our efforts to urge more unity among the countries of Western Europe to the extent it is possible. If Russia should attack we certainly want as unified a defense as possible. It is encouraging that in this field General Eisenhower by the force of his personality has made so much headway in persuading the European nations of the tremendous importance of arming themselves in a joint defense.

The point I wish to make is that our relations with each of these countries require a different approach and different treatment. We cannot blithely say, "Western Europe should do that," "Western Europe thinks this."

The questions we have to meet with respect to Europe may be classified as follows:

1. Shall we give large financial economic aid to European countries out of taxes levied on the American taxpayer?

2. Shall we give arms, equipment, and supplies from the

same source to arm these countries and to encourage them to arm themselves?

3. Shall we agree to go to their defense if they are attacked by Russia or anyone else?

4. Shall we commit American troops in time of peace to an international army to be stationed in Europe?

Those who desire to commit American troops to Europe in time of peace have talked a good deal about our running out on Europe, if we refuse to follow their policy. I think it ought to be pointed out that we have given billions for the purposes of financial economic aid, we have given billions for arms, equipment, and supplies, and we have definitely agreed to go to the defense of these countries if they are attacked. The sum of all this is probably the greatest support that one nation has ever given to other nations in the history of the world, and if a war actually occurred we probably would be supplying at least half of the total support for that war, even if we sent no troops whatsoever.

In the field of economic aid we have been committing billions of our taxpayers' money since the war. Following lend-lease, we supported various minor projects, including UNRAA; then we committed some six billion dollars to the two Bretton Woods projects. We extended a loan of four billion to Great Britain. We are carrying through the Marshall Plan at a total cost of something in the neighborhood of fifteen billion. All of this aid has been extended to Western Europe out of all proportion to our aid to the rest of the world. A great deal of this aid was extended long before we had any realization of the threat from Soviet Russia, although most of the Marshall aid was justified on that ground. Before the Russian threat I was very dubious about the policy of advancing money to Europe in such large amounts, certainly when General Marshall proposed to include Soviet Russia. The European countries are fully developed countries. The idea of extending large gifts from one country to another was certainly a novel one, and if the world had faced a peaceful solution it might well have been that these countries could have achieved a sounder recovery, although a slower one, by working out their own problems. Certainly it is unwise for any nation to become dependent upon the charity of another nation, and it is just as bad for the country receiving the charity as it is costly to the country which gives it.

The question today, however, is hardly an issue on which there is a serious split. Once the Russian threat was apparent I was in favor of the Marshall Plan, in order that these countries might be able to meet communism more swiftly and effectively. Our assistance undoubtedly enabled them to recover in three or four years to a point which they might not have reached without our aid for perhaps ten years. Time was important in the fight against communism, and the assistance we gave enabled some of these countries to bring about a recovery, wherein communism found a much less fertile soil. But in 1951 the Western European countries have recovered, and their production in most cases far exceeds their prewar production. Aid of this kind today is far more justified to meet a famine in India or an influx of immigration in Israel than it is to support a European country able to support itself. The Administration and Paul Hoffman himself have always emphasized that the Marshall Plan aid was to end in 1952, and even such extension as the Administration proposes today seems to be simply an incident to the arms aid in which we are now involved.

With regard to the giving of arms aid at the expense of the American taxpayer, I believe that this general policy is correct, subject to certain conditions. In the first place, it ought to be fairly clear that the nations to which aid is extended are really threatened by Communist attack. I have never favored the giving of arms aid indiscriminately to South American countries. In the second place, the amount must be within the capacity of the United States to include in its budget and in its program of production. In the third place, I do not think arms aid should be given in such a way as to lead Russia to believe that an attack is contemplated against Russia itself and so incite it to a war which it might not otherwise undertake.

I supported the bills for the arming of Greece and Turkey. I am quite willing to support arms aid to Great Britain and France to the extent that they are not able to arm themselves, although the providing of such arms should be a first call on their own budgets, and arms aid should not be provided by the United States simply to prevent some slight reduction in their civilian standard of living. We ourselves are contemplating such a reduction because of our own arms program, and I see no reason why the other nations should not be prepared to make the same sacrifice. In fact, unless they are going to give that much importance to their own defense it is unlikely that when the time comes there will be any wholehearted participation in that defense.

We should long ago have supplied much greater support in the matter of arms and equipment to the Nationalist Government of China. We should never have left Korea until the Korean Army was fully armed against a possible attack by the North Koreans. We have finally adopted the policy of arming the Chinese Nationalists on Formosa. But whether we are doing it is another question. In this field, as in all other fields of aid, Europe has had the lion's share of our assistance, and the importance of Europe has been fully recognized in that program and in the military aid which we are now contemplating.

When we come to the third and fourth proposals to assist Europe, however, we enter a much more controversial field, because under both of these proposals we frankly commit the United States to war in case Russia attacks. This we have not done anywhere else in the world, except as to the island nations of Japan, the Philippine Republic, Australia and New Zealand. The Atlantic Pact definitely commits us to go to the defense of any one of the eleven nations if Russia or anyone else attacks those nations.

There are various reasons why this should be done. We became involved in Europe by fighting World War II, so that we could not remove ourselves from the situation even if we wanted to. We are one of the occupying powers in Germany, and no one has yet been able to devise a method by which we can withdraw from that obligation without practically inviting the communization of Germany. We have several divisions of troops in Germany, and if a war arose we would inevitably be involved in that war.

We have an obligation to see that Germany itself does not rearm in such a manner as to become again a threat to the security of Europe and of the world. Senator Vandenberg proposed to Russia that we join in a more or less indefinite occupation of Germany to the extent necessary to prevent the development of another aggressive Germany, hoping by that means to allay the fears of Russia of another German invasion. I thoroughly approved the policy of saying to Germany that certain limitations must be imposed upon its economy, to prevent the development of dangerous arms, and backing up that assertion by undertaking to move soldiers into Germany the moment that the limitations were exceeded. It was the failure of Great Britain and France to take similar action to enforce the Treaty of Versailles that brought about the success of Hitler in the invasion of the Rhineland and his gradual emancipation from all limitation.

Therefore it seemed to me wise to notify Russia definitely that if they undertook such a war they would find themselves at war with the United States. This feature of the Atlantic Pact was, in fact, the extension of the Monroe Doctrine to Europe. The Monroe Doctrine brought peace to the American continent for a hundred years. A notification of this kind to Russia seems to me a very clear deterrent to its beginning a war, because it must necessarily fear the bombing by the United States which would result if they began aggression against members of the pact. I do not like the obligation written into the pact which binds us for twenty years to come to the defense of any country, no matter by whom it is attacked and even though the aggressor may be another member of the pact; and I do not like the obligation of the pact which requires us to go to the assistance of a nation attacked, without any consultation with other persons, without a decision by a majority of those involved, and without any examination of the reasons for the aggression which may have occurred. Nevertheless, I think the advantage of the notice given to Russia outweighs, at least for the present, these excessive obligations of the pact into which we have entered.

In spite of the fact that I approved the warning given to Russia by the ratification of the Atlantic Pact, I voted against it because I felt it was contrary to the whole theory of the United Nations Charter, which had not then been shown to be ineffective, because I felt that it might develop aggressive features more likely to incite Russia to war than to deter it from war, and because I thought that, at least by implication, it committed the United States to the policy of a land war in Europe, when me might find that a third world war could better be fought by other means.

I wish to make it clear that once the United States has entered into an obligation I am in favor of meeting every such obligation. I do feel that the making of this pact was a clear recognition of the ineffectiveness of the United Nations against Russian aggression, and a violation of its spirit if not its language. The pact apparently is not made under Articles 52 to 54, inclusive, because we do not propose to consult the Security Council as there contemplated, we do plan to take enforcement action without the authorization of the Security Council, and we do not plan to keep it fully informed. The pact must, therefore, be supported under Article 51 alone, which says:

Nothing in the present Charter shall impair the inherent right of individual or collective self-defense if an armed attack occurs against a member of the United Nations, until the Security Council has taken the measures necessary to maintain international peace and security.

It seems clear to me, however, that the right is to be exercised only "if an armed attack occurs." I do not think Article 51 contemplates that one nation can agree to send troops to other nations prior to the occurrence of such an attack. An undertaking by the most powerful nation in the world to arm half the world against the other half goes far beyond any "right of collective self-defense if an armed attack occurs." It violates the whole spirit of the United Nations Charter. That charter looks to the reduction of armaments by agreement between individual nations. The Atlantic Pact moves in exactly the opposite direction from the purposes of the charter and makes a farce of further efforts to secure international peace through law and justice. It necessarily divides the world into two armed camps. It may be said that the world is already so divided, but it cannot be said that by emphasizing that division we are carrying out the spirit of the United Nations.

With the obligation to provide arms in the pact it is even more clear that the pact is a military alliance, a treaty by which one nation undertakes to arm half the European world against the other half. It cannot be described otherwise than as a military alliance. Of course, it is not like some of the alliances in the past, although many of them, such as the Franco-British Alliance prior to World War I, were entirely defensive in character, or purported to be. Others were offensive and defensive alliances. I quite agree that the purpose of this alliance is not offensive, and that we have no offensive purpose in mind. But it is exactly like many military alliances of the past.

I was not impressed by General Bradley's effort to distinguish this military alliance from others. He said:

As I see it, the purpose and meaning of this is entirely different from the normal military alliances as we have known them in years past. Here we are binding ourselves together with some other nations who have free institutions and ideals like our own. Some of the military alliances in the past were a combination of people who did not have such common ideals. Some of them were for purposes of offense, some for defense, that is true.

In other words, the general's argument is that this is not a military alliance because all of its members are virtuous—for the moment.

While this is not an offensive alliance, the line between defense and offense today is indeed a shadowy one. The Maginot Line was the essence of pure defense. Today it is the target of ridicule. Every good defense includes elements of offense. We cannot have an adequate armament for defense which cannot be converted overnight into a weapon of offense, at least for limited objectives. We talked of defense for some years before entering World War II, while our preparation was also for offense. The result is that, no matter how defensive an alliance may be, if it carries the obligation to arm it means the building up of competitive offensive armament. This treaty, therefore, means inevitably an armament race, and armament races in the past have led to war.

Nevertheless after the Korean and Chinese episodes we have to give up the idea of the enforcement of peace by the United Nations, and I see no choice now except to rely on our armed forces and alliances with those nations willing to fight the advance of communism. But don't let's fool ourselves into regarding a military alliance as a world state based on the ideals of collective security.

At the time the Pact was being considered I also felt that it was likely to incite Russia to start a war because of the threat involved to its satellite countries and therefore to its own safety. There was bound to be a period during which that threat would be apparent, and Western Europe would still be wholly unarmed. Mr. John Foster Dulles shared this view in warning against the inclusion of Norway in the Pact. He said on March 8, 1950:

"While the Soviet Government has no present intention of resorting to war as an instrument of national policy, nevertheless it can be assumed the Soviet state would use the Red Army if its leaders felt that their homeland was imminently and seriously threatened."

I have no means of guessing whether the Russians intend to start a third world war or not, but if they do intend to do so I believe they will begin that war, regardless of anything we do, when they feel that the time is most propitious from their own standpoint. If they do not have the intention of starting a third world war, then I believe there is only one incitement on our part which might lead them to change their minds and begin such a war. That would be the creation of a condition in which Russia feared the actual invasion of Russia or invasion of some satellite country sufficiently close as to threaten the future invasion of Russia. However, my fears do not seem to have been borne out up to this time. Either the Russians are very much afraid of starting a third world war, or they see serious weaknesses in their position which can only be remedied in time, or they don't regard the European Army in its present condition as likely to be a threat to anyone for some years to come. Their failure to move in Europe, or with Russian armies anywhere, raises the hope that perhaps we have completely overestimated the Russian strength. Unfortunately we cannot take a chance.

We have no choice now except to complete as rapidly as possible the arming of Western Europe if it desires to be armed. That is the policy decided on in the Atlantic Pact, and I am in favor of carrying out this commitment, as worked out by the Council and General Eisenhower under the Pact.

In the beginning of 1951, however, we were suddenly committed to a new project, without any consultation with Congress and without any justification from the terms of the Atlantic Pact. That is the program to build up a great international army on the continent of Europe with a substantial commitment of American land troops.

I think it should be made clear, first, that this was in no way contemplated by the Atlantic Pact and that the United States is in no way obligated to engage in any such project because of the ratification of the Atlantic Pact. The proposal violates the general principles of foreign policy which I have advocated, but I do feel that the special situation of Europe justifies the stationing of a limited number of American troops on the continent of Europe. I believe it should be limited and that no further commitment should be made beyond the six divisions already promised, without a thorough reconsideration of the whole policy and definite further action by Congress itself.

The first question is to determine exactly what the project is and whether it is authorized by the Atlantic Pact. Article 9 of the North Atlantic Treaty reads as follows:

The parties hereby establish a council, on which each of them shall be represented, to consider matters concerning the implementation of this treaty. . . . The council . . . shall establish immediately a defense committee which shall recommend measures for the implementation of Articles 3 and 5.

The report of the Senate Foreign Relations Committee says that the powers of the council "are purely advisory with respect to governmental action. Its purpose is to make recommendations to the governments and to assist them in reaching coordinated decisions. It should be emphasized, however, that the responsibility for making decisions lies in the respective governments rather than in the councils. . . . The defense committee will concern itself primarily with making plans and recommendations for the implementation of Articles 3 and 5, i.e., preparation for the exercise of the inherent right of individual or collective self-defense. Being subordinate to the council, it too shall have only advisory powers."

In December 1950 the council established under Article 9 met in Brussels and issued the following communiqué on December 19:

The North Atlantic Council, acting on the recommendations of its defense committee, today completed arrangements initiated in September last for the establishment in Europe of an integrated force under a centralized control and command. This force is to be composed of contingents contributed by the participating governments.

The North Atlantic Council speaks as if it had authority to do this, although its recommendations under the treaty are only advisory.

On December 22 Secretary Acheson made the following statement about the Brussels agreement:

At Brussels we did several things. We took recommendations which had come from the meetings immediately preceding in London and acted on those recommendations. They had to do with the creation of the united, unified, integrated army which is to provide for the defense of Europe. The papers which came to us laid out the structure of that army, how it should be composed, of what troops, where the troops should come from, how it should be organized, its command structure, the higher command structure which would give that army its direction, and how the supreme commander should be selected and appointed. We dealt with and acted upon all those matters.

The structure was agreed upon, and the force was created.

I cannot understand what authority Secretary Acheson had in that connection, because the Council's power was only advisory; but that is the statement which he issued.

After this subject began to be debated in Congress, however, it assumed a much more indefinite aspect. It was denied that there was any commitment whatever on our part or, apparently, on the part of any other nation. In all the extended hearings Congress was unable to obtain any reliable information as to the size of the "united, unified, integrated army which is to provide for the defense of Europe." It was unable to find out how many American divisions were to be contributed under the program referred to by Secretary Acheson. The request of the Administration finally boiled down to a desire to send four more divisions to Europe to support the two divisions already in occupied Germany. It was never made clear whether these divisions were permanently assigned to an international army or whether we were at liberty to withdraw them at any time. It was never made clear whether they would take orders only from General Eisenhower, acting under the orders of a twelve-nation council, or whether they would take orders from the Defense Department in the United States. It is uncertain whether General Eisenhower can overrule the Joint Chiefs of Staff on questions of military strategy or whether they are to be superior to him.

I could only come to the conclusion that there was in existence a perfectly definite project, probably calling for a good many more than six American divisions and probably providing for an army of fifty or sixty divisions over-all. No nation perhaps committed itself unequivocally to this project. Congress could never obtain from General Marshall any definite statement that six divisions were the limit of an American contribution in time of peace, and in view of the past history of the Administration it is reasonable to feel that in another year we will be asked for more divisions to carry out this original plan. The Senate finally dealt with the situation by approving the general contribution of six divisions to Europe but indicating that the President should return to Congress for authority to commit any larger army to the continent of Europe in time of peace.

There is nothing in the Atlantic Treaty which authorizes this international army in Europe in time of peace to which American troops are to be committed.

Article 5 of the treaty reads:

The parties agree that an armed attack against one or more of them in Europe or North America shall be considered an attack against them all; and consequently they agree that, if such an armed attack occurs, each of them, in exercise of the right of individual or collective self-defense recognized by Article 51 of the Charter of the United Nations, will assist the party or parties so attacked by taking forthwith, individually and in concert with the other parties, such action as it deems necessary, including the use of armed force, to restore and maintain the security of the North Atlantic area.

By its terms this Article clearly leaves us free to determine what action we deem necessary. In other words, we are obligated to go to the assistance of any member attacked by Russia, but we certainly are free to determine how we shall fight that war. A council is set up by Article 9, which is to recommend measures for the implementation of Article 5, but we are certainly not bound to accept any such recommendations.

In July 1949 on the floor of the Senate it was even argued that the pact did not obligate us to provide arms and equipment for the parties in the pact. The amount of this equipment, however, was not to be extensive, and certainly it was based on a very large contribution by the other parties to their defense. Senator Vandenberg severely limited even our contributions for arms. He explained in the debate on the bill implementing the pact that the over-all assistance was only $1,130,-000,000, to be paid out at the rate of about $500,000,000 a year. The senator from Texas (Mr. Connally) made it clear that the pact did not obligate us to send a land army to Europe. He said:

This bill does not provide, as has been said by some persons, that we are rearming Western Europe. Western Europe will spend $5 or $6 for each dollar contributed by the United States. Let me point out that we are not increasing by this aid the number of armed men in the armies of the North Atlantic Pact nations. We are simply undertaking to modernize their existing armies which they themselves raise by aiding them in obtaining equipment, munitions, and supplies. But we are not sending a single soldier to any of those countries for combat purposes, nor are we insisting that they increase the size of their armed forces.

So it can be seen that what was proposed at Brussels is something entirely different from what was being considered when we adopted the Atlantic Pact.

In his appearances before the Foreign Relations Committee,

Secretary Acheson denied that we were obligated to send troops or even extensive aid in equipment. He said:

It is not proposed to increase the establishments beyond what is already provided in their budgets.

In 1951 we are urging that they triple and quadruple their budgets. I quote further from Secretary Acheson:

So far as the pact countries are concerned, United States assistance will be somewhere between one sixth and one seventh of the total effort which will go into military efforts in Europe. We will provide, as is stated in the statement, approximately $1,130,-000,000 for the pact countries.

In 1951 we are talking about providing six and one quarter billion dollars' worth of arms aid this year and twenty-five billions in three years and, in addition, from 10 per cent to 25 per cent of all the foot soldiers involved in a European defense army.

In committee, Secretary Acheson was asked the direct question by the Senator from Iowa (Mr. Hickenlooper):

I believe you said earlier in your testimony today that it was contemplated that a great portion of the armament, or the developed armament, of Western Europe, in the nations of this pact, would be carried under their own weight. I presume that that refers also to the manpower in their armies. I am interested in getting the answers as to whether or not we are expected to supply substantial numbers—by that, I do not mean a thousand or two, or five hundred, or anything of that kind, but very substantial numbers—of troops and troop organizations, of American troops, to implement the land power of Western Europe prior to aggression.

Is that contemplated under Article 3, where we agree to maintain and develop the collective capacity to resist? In other words, are we going to be expected to send substantial numbers of troops over there as a more or less permanent contribution to the development of these countries' capacity to resist?

Secretary Acheson: The answer to that question, Senator, is a clear and absolute "No."

Since the sponsors of the treaty, backed by the State Department, took this position, they can hardly contend now that we have any obligation under the Atlantic Pact to send American soldiers to Europe.

We did have warning at the time of the Atlantic Pact that the military authorities in the Pentagon regarded the pact as leading toward a land war with Russia in Europe. I pointed out, in opposing the pact, that we were headed in this direction. I said:

It is one thing to agree to go to war with Russia if it attacks Western Europe. It is another to send American ground troops to defend Norway or Denmark or Holland or Italy, or even France and England. I cannot assert positively that we are committing ourselves to a particular type of war, but I am inclined to think that we are. Thus General Bradley testified before the committee:

"Finally, after studied appraisal of the future security provisions for our country, the Joint Chiefs of Staff are in unanimous agreement that our strategy, in case we are attacked, must rely on sufficient integrated forces of land, sea, and air power to carry the war back to the aggressor, ultimately subjugating the sources of his military and industrial power. Plans for the common defense of the existing free world must provide for the security of Western Europe without abandoning these countries to the terrors of another enemy occupation. Only upon that premise can nations closest to the frontiers be expected to stake their fortunes with ours in the common defense."

This appeared to contemplate the use of American armies in a land war with Russia on the continent of Europe the day after war starts. It appeared to contemplate later an invasion along the lines which Napoleon and Hitler found to be impossible. It implied that the nations which signed this pact expect us to send American troops to defend their frontiers.

But it was only our military planners who discussed sending American land troops to Europe. Responsible officials of the Government absolutely repudiated any idea that the Atlantic Pact contemplated any such aid.

I did not think we should force our assistance on any nation which does not really wish to arm itself. I did not think we should insist that the European nations form a great international army, unless they take the initiative and request us to help them in that project. If these nations really do desire to build up their own arms and if it appears that that defense has a reasonable chance of success I believe we should commit some limited number of American divisions to work with them to show that we are not evading the toughest part of the defense program provided by the Atlantic Pact. Such a program, however, never ought to be a key point in our strictly American military strategy. And the initiative should be theirs and not ours.

I have also viewed the proposed European-army project with concern, because I believe it is likely to grow beyond the capacity of the United States and therefore to threaten its entire economic structure. I have favored sending four more divisions to Europe, although it should be noted that our six divisions there will be one fourth of the total number of American divisions contemplated by the very extensive and expensive plan recommended by the President and the Joint Chiefs of Staff. But the setting up of this army under the command of an American general, the initiative which we have taken, and the tremendous emphasis placed by the Chiefs of Staff on the conducting of a land war in Europe—all, I am afraid, may commit us, before we get through, to far more than six divisions. In World War II we had sixty divisions in Europe.

I have shown that the program recommended by the President is at the very limit of or beyond our economic capacity. Yet this program only contemplates an American land Army of twenty-four divisions, obviously insufficient to control the land in Europe and Asia. With the men proposed for the Air Force and Navy we can apparently achieve a reasonably complete control of sea and air. On the other hand, the control of the Eurasian Continent would require at least a quadrupling of the expense for the Army. If we commit ourselves without limitation to the European project we will be faced with the constant effort to increase the Army and the tremendous expense involved in that effort. There is practically no limit to the size or expense of the type of army which ultimately would undertake to win a war against Russia on the continent of Asia and in Russia itself. We are, of course, interested in the defense of Western Europe, but it is beyond our capacity unless the Europeans provide not only the bulk of the troops but also the bulk of the interest and initiative, and finally take over the responsibility.

General Eisenhower has made progress in persuading the European Pact members that their own safety depends on arming themselves adequately in a united defense against possible Russian attack. Certainly a Western Europe adequately armed and prepared to meet any Russian military threat is a tremendous addition to the security of the United States. I have said that I think it justifies our temporary contribution of some American divisions to stimulate that effort. Our aim should be to make Europe sufficiently strong so that American troops can be withdrawn from the continent of Europe.

I am concerned about the serious danger of committing our greatest efforts to a land war on the continent of Europe against Russia. The program which the Administration is pursuing apparently contemplates that we send, or promise to send, to Europe within a few weeks of the beginning of the war enough American troops to defend the pact countries including Norway, Denmark, Holland, Belgium and Italy. I do not believe we can prepare in time of peace for any such project without straining our economic ability beyond the limit. We also risk the loss of a war, a loss which in the end might threaten the very security of the United States itself. Neither Napoleon nor Hitler was ever able finally to defeat Russia on land, although each had more men than we are now planning to provide, certainly in comparison to the number of Russians then available. Our men will certainly be outnumbered as they were in Korea, where we almost suffered a disastrous defeat. Our defense against Russian hordes apparently depends on the development of new weapons, which are still untested. Even then a modern war cannot be won by remaining on the defensive, even behind a Maginot Line of bazookas.

I somewhat doubt whether the Russians really can deliver an atomic bomb. Nevertheless, we are proposing to spend some three billion dollars building air shelters in this country to protect our people and cities against Russian atom bombs delivered all the way from Russia itself. If that is a possibility, then surely there is danger that the Russians can destroy all of the ports our Army may be using on the continent. They may be able to prevent the landing of troops and the furnishing of adequate supplies. They might even make a Dunkerque escape impossible. One atom bomb at Hungnam might have destroyed the entire American force which escaped so successfully from there.

In my opinion we are completely able to defend the United States itself. The one great danger we face is that we may overcommit ourselves in this battle against Russia. Germany lies in ruins today because Hitler thought he could conquer the world when he had no such ability. Italy is a poverty-stricken nation because Mussolini thought that he could create an Italian empire. An unwise and overambitious foreign policy, and particularly the effort to do more than we are able to do, is the one thing which might in the end destroy our armies and prove a real threat to the liberty of the people of the United States.

In conclusion, let me say that no one is more determined to resist Communist aggression in the world than I am. I think the Russians present a menace to the liberty of the entire world and to our way of life, a menace greater than we have faced before in our history. That menace is not entirely military. It is a battle of liberty against communism in the minds of men.

We cannot afford to destroy at home the very liberty which we must sell to the rest of the world as the basis for progress and happiness.

There is no reason whatever for panic or defeatism. I feel less concern about the ultimate success of Russian military power than do many others. But if Russia chooses to start a war it will be a long and bitter conflict, and this country must remain strong in every aspect of production and morale. Our limited resources must be directed to the field where they can be most effective. I do not believe that Western Europe can be defended unless the Western Europeans are determined to defend themselves and will take the initiative in the rearming which is essential for that purpose. To encourage that action we are furnishing them with economic assistance and military equipment in practically any amount they can use. We will support them by sea and by air, and I would agree to send some troops to prove to them that we do intend to fight at their side if Russia attacks. But even the program which I outline will require tremendous sacrifices from the American people, from every taxpayer, from every family, from every boy. We should not further endanger the position of America as the arsenal of democracy and the bastion of liberty.

7. The Russian Menace. How Do We Meet It in the Far East?

AS EUROPE requires special consideration, so also the peculiar position of Korea justifies us in considering whether an exception should have been made to the general principle of not committing troops to the continent of Asia. Korea does occupy a very strategic position, and a complete domination of Korea by the Russian Communists would certainly be a threat to the security of Japan. The Administration decided, however, that it would withdraw all troops from Korea and would not undertake to defend Korea by the use of American soldiers. As a long-term policy this was generally in accord with the principles I have outlined. Because of the importance of Korea, however, there should have been no question that the situation demanded all-out arms aid to provide the South Koreans with a complete defense against attack from the north. Perhaps it even justified a definite notification, at least to the North Koreans, that if they chose to attack they would find themselves at war with the United States and that we would return with sea and air forces to fight that war. But the Administration not only failed to adopt either of these two policies, but it went very much further in a definite statement of policy by Secretary Acheson in January 1950, saying that except for Japan, Okinawa and the Philippines we could not assure the rest of the

Far East against attack. I believe that our Government invited the invasion of Korea by the weakness of its policy in these respects.

At the time we withdrew from Korea we declared that we would give armed assistance to Korea. The Mutual Defense Assistance Act of 1949 authorized the President to furnish military assistance to South Korea. Assistant Secretary Webb, of the State Department, testified specifically before both House and Senate committees that the appropriation sought was for the purpose of helping the Koreans to fight external aggression. The bill was passed in October 1949. By June 1950 not a single bit of aid had been given, except merely some small arms that had been left behind when we withdrew from Korea. So far as I can discover, the South Koreans were never given any airplanes, tanks, or heavy artillery.

Apparently someone in the State Department had changed the policy of giving the South Koreans sufficient arms with which to deter external aggression. The President admitted later, in his statement about Korea, that the Government forces of Korea were armed only to "prevent border raids and preserve internal security." Perhaps the policy was changed because someone was afraid that if the South Koreans had tanks and airplanes they would attack the North Korean Communists. Therefore, we gave them only small arms, which would be useless for offense and also for defense if the North Koreans attacked them. It was certainly a weak policy. To what extent it was again the result of a deliberate policy of not antagonizing the Communists in Asia, it is difficult to say at the moment.

The Russians certainly read what Senator Connally said on May 5, 1950, only a month before the Korean War. He was asked the following question on the questionnaire appearing in United States News and World Report:

"Do you think the suggestion that we abandon South Korea is going to be seriously considered?"

The Chairman of the Foreign Relations Committee of the Senate replied:

"I am afraid it is going to be seriously considered because I'm afraid it's going to happen, whether we want it to or not. I'm for Korea. We're trying to help her—we're appropriating money now to help her. But South Korea is cut right across this line—north of it are the Communists, with access to the mainland—and Russia is over there on the mainland. So that whenever she takes a notion she can just overrun Korea, just like she will probably overrun Formosa when she gets ready to do it. I hope not, of course."

The next question was:

"But isn't Korea an essential part of the defense strategy?"

The answer of the Senator from Texas was:

"No. Of course, any position like that is of some strategic importance. But I don't think it is very greatly important. It has been testified before us that Japan, Okinawa, and the Philippines make the chain of defense which is absolutely necessary. And, of course, any additional territory along in that area would be that much more, but it's not absolutely essential."

So both the chairman of the Foreign Relations Committee and the Secretary of State said, in effect, to the North Koreans: "We are not going to interfere in South Korea. We have moved out of South Korea. It is indefensible anyway. We are not coming back. We do not propose to give South Korea any arms of a character useful in modern war."

That was a direct invitation to the North Koreans to attack. It was an invitation to Soviet Russia to believe, as it did, that here was a soft spot where communism could move in without difficulty. I think the policy, or lack of policy, of the administration brought on the Korean War. If we had taken a definite position as to South Korea I believe there would not have been an aggression. If we had simply warned the North Koreans that an attack by them meant a war with America I believe there would not have been the attack which took place.

For two hundred years Russia has been moving forward by going into soft spots. That has been its policy. Wherever it thought it could grab something and get away with it, it has done so. Here was a place which the Secretary of State and the chairman of the Foreign Relations Committee gave the Russians every reason to consider a soft spot.

Then the President, on June 25, 1950, in one of those spasmodic actions which are more or less characteristic of this administration, entirely reversed the American policy which he had previously announced. When he moved into Korea after the North Koreans attacked I had much sympathy with his reversal of position. I stated on June 28, 1950, after American armed forces had been moved into Korea:

The time had to come, sooner or later, when we would give definite notice to the Communists that a move beyond a declared line would result in war. That has been the policy which we have adopted in Europe. Whether the President has chosen the right time or the right place to declare this policy may be open to question. He has information which I do not have.

It seems to me that the new policy is adopted at an unfortunate time and involves a very difficult military operation indeed—the defense of Korea. I sincerely hope that our armed forces may be successful in Korea. I sincerely hope that the policy thus adopted will not lead to war with Russia. In any event, I believe the general principle of the policy is right, and I see no choice except to back up wholeheartedly and with every available resource the men in our armed forces who have been moved into Korea.

If we are going to defend Korea, it seems to me that we should have retained our armed forces there and should have given, a year ago, the notice which the President has given today. With such a policy there never would have been such an attack by the North Koreans.

We went into Korea on the theory that the United Nations was going to punish aggression in order to prevent aggression in the future. I think it is a sound principle, if you have an international organization with the ability to do the job. The difficulty is that we were relying upon a weak reed in the United Nations. The United Nations Charter is so weak, with the provision for the veto, that as a matter of fact there is no legal means of preventing aggression. The only reason we happened to secure action in one case for one moment was that the Russians were not present. We went in knowing full well that all future action taken by the United Nations would be subject to the Russian veto when the Russians returned to the Security Council.

We went in with the possibility facing us that there might be further aggression and knowing that then we could not rely on the United Nations. So we went in. We got little aid from other members of the United Nations. Our own forces were so weak and limited that the country we were saving from aggression was practically destroyed. We were successful in defeating the North Koreans but when we were almost at the point of occupying the entire country we were attacked by the Chinese, in November 1950.

That was the second aggression. The theory of our Korean action would require, as a matter of moral principle, that we then throw all the forces of the United Nations against the Chinese aggressors, defeat them, and march to Peiping. Unfortunately, that was an impossible policy for two reasons. The United Nations would not do it, because the Russians in the Security Council vetoed the action. Even the General Assembly, which has no power to call any member to act or provide armed forces, took a long time merely to declare that the Chinese Communists were aggressors, which was obvious from the very moment they moved into Korea. In the second place, it was a wholly impossible military operation, to carry out against a big aggressor the kind of action which we carried out against a little aggressor. So we had been sucked into something which was more than we could undertake, and we found ourselves in an extremely unfortunate situation.

Underlying the whole situation is our policy toward Formosa. The only logical application of the broad general principles, which I have advocated and which we have followed in Europe, for meeting the Communist threat is to undertake to defend Formosa if the Chinese Nationalist Government desires assistance. Here is an island, more than a hundred miles off the coast of China, which is entirely easy to defend against any Communist attack, with practically no cost to the United States. Yet in January 1950 Secretary Acheson warned the American people that they must be prepared for the taking over of Formosa by the Chinese Communists, and he stated unequivocally that we would not undertake any defense of Formosa. I believe this attitude grew out of the pro-Communist policy of the Far Eastern Division of the State Department and the Secretary's strong prejudices against doing anything to help Chiang Kai-shek. Both Secretaries Acheson and Marshall seem to have a vested interest in the mistakes which they made in China in earlier days, and they are very loath to adopt any policy which will cast doubt on the correctness of their action at that time.

Apparently, it was General MacArthur's remarks on the subject of the strategic position of Formosa and the need of defending it which from time to time aroused the Secretary of State and the President to a violent indignation against the general. If we really mean our anti-Communist policy it seems obvious to me that we should have backed the Chinese Nationalists in past years and should back them today on Formosa. If there is any chance of their regaining their influence in South China it seems obvious that we should not fail to support them in that action also, so long as it does not involve the use of American troops on the mainland.

Once it became apparent that the policy of punishing aggression could not be carried through there was some logical argument for entirely evacuating Korea. But having gone into Korea, having suffered more than a hundred thousand casualties, it seems obvious to me that we could not withdraw. Such a withdrawal would be interpreted throughout Asia not only as a political defeat but also as a military defeat. It would have been an admission that we have completely wasted all the effort and the lives which have been devoted to the Korean adventure. There seemed to be no choice except to see it through.

Since it was impossible to invade China, the best solution would have been to drive the Chinese out of Korea, to ask the United Nations to set up a Korean Republic, to maintain our troops there for some time and then arm the Koreans with weapons which would enable them to stand against Chinese attack, and to give them such economic and arms aid in peace and military aid from the sea and air in war as we might be able to afford. The Administration, however, refused to use the various measures suggested by General MacArthur as a means of conquering all of Korea and setting up an independent Republic under the protection of the United Nations. Their only proposal was a more or less endless war in which we would advance to the Thirty-eighth Parallel but would not attempt to go beyond that point to any material extent. Such a stalemate accomplished no purpose, except to eliminate the idea that we had suffered a military defeat.

The only other policy under consideration, prior to the Malik proposal for an armistice, was the negotiating of an armistice with the North Koreans and the Chinese Communists, the withdrawal of all foreign troops from Korea, and the discussion of the questions of Formosa and the admission of Chinese Communists to the United Nations and to the negotiations on the Japanese Peace Treaty. Such a settlement, I believe, would be very much worse even than an unconditional withdrawal from Korea, but the State Department at one time approved it. In January 1951 the Secretary of State agreed to the cease-fire plan approved by the United Nations political committee. That cease-fire plan provided, first, for a truce. Then it provided:

To permit the carrying out of the General Assembly resolution that Korea should be a unified, independent, democratic, sovereign State with a constitution and a government based on free popular elections, all non-Korean armed forces will be withdrawn, by appropriate stages, from Korea, and appropriate arrangements, in accordance with United Nations principles, will be made for the Korean people to express their own free will in respect to their future government.

The withdrawal of all non-Korean forces from Korea under the conditions existing there would, in my opinion, mean the communization of Korea. The Russians do not care what they do underground. They do not regard their promises. Our effort in a Korean election of that kind would be completely swamped by Communist machinations. In effect, to agree to that is to agree to a Communist-controlled government of Korea.

Then, even more important, there was contained in the agreement the following:

As soon as the agreement has been reached on a cease-fire, the General Assembly shall set up an appropriate body which shall include representatives of the governments of the United Kingdom, the United States of America, the Union of Soviet Socialist Republics, and the People's Republic of China with a view to the achievement of a settlement, in conformity with existing international obligations and provisions of the United Nations Charter, of far-eastern problems, including among others, those of Formosa and of representation of China in the United Nations.

Thus, as late as January 1951 the Secretary of State agreed that we would sit down with England, with Communist China itself, with the Union of Soviet Socialist Republics, all three of them urging upon us appeasement peace, and that there would be completely excluded from the conference Nationalist China, the recognized Government of China, which has a seat in the Security Council today. That was equivalent to saying, "We are willing to give up Formosa. We are willing to have Communist China admitted to the United Nations." It was fortunate indeed that Communist China declined to accept that cease-fire proposal. The Department of State came out with the naïve statement that it had agreed to the proposal because it felt all the time that Communist China probably would not accept it and so it would give us a certain practical advantage with the United Nations.

At the time of writing, the military commanders are negotiating an armistice. Certainly it is better to maintain an uneasy peace on the Thirty-eighth Parallel than a policy of perpetual war on the Thirty-eighth Parallel. But an armistice is likely to leave us in approximately the same position we were in two years ago, before we moved American troops out of South Korea, except that we would have to put up billions of dollars to repair the destruction in South Korea. Is any such expenditure justified, until a real peace is finally negotiated with Soviet Russia? Is this armistice to lead to negotiations that would have all the faults of the cease-fire agreement of January 1951?

Regardless of the matter of an armistice, if we really believe in a policy of containing communism there is no logical reason why we should not give a hundred per cent support to the Chinese Nationalist Government on Formosa and reject any idea whatever of a compromise on this issue. There is no reason why we should agree to the admission of the Chinese Communists to the United Nations or to the negotiations with Japan for a permanent peace. It would be far better to withdraw without condition from Korea itself, without compromising ourselves on these other issues, than to follow the general proposals along the line of those made by the United Nations in January 1951.

It has been suggested that there is a fundamental issue between those who think that Europe is more important and those who think that Asia is more important. Certainly my position is not an extreme one on the subject of Asia. I only insist that we apply to Asia the same basic policy which we apply to Europe. As I have said, that policy is to check communism at every possible point where it is within our capacity to do so.

Broadly speaking, my quarrel is with those who wish to go all-out in Europe, even beyond our capacity, and who at the same time refuse to apply our general program and strategy to the Far East. In Greece we moved in with overwhelming support for the Greek Government, even though it at first had strong reactionary tendencies. We gave it hundreds of millions of dollars to suppress Communists within the country. But in China we hampered the Nationalist Government. We tried to force it to take Communists into the Cabinet. The State Department spoke of Communists as agrarian reformers and cut off arms from the Nationalist Government at the most crucial time. Contrary to the whole theory of the containment of communism, where it could be done without serious cost or danger, the Administration proposed to surrender Formosa to the Communists and has constantly flirted with that idea.

Even though we were engaged in a bitter and dangerous war, the Administration refused to fight that war with all the means at its command, on the theory that we might incite Russia to start a third world war. But in Europe we have not hesitated to risk a third world war over and over again. When we moved into Greece to support the Government the Russians might have moved in to support the Communists. The building up of a Turkish Army and Air Force within easy reach of Moscow is far more of a threat to Russia than the bombing of Chinese supply lines in Manchuria. In Europe we have not hesitated to say to Russia, "If you cross certain lines and attack any one of eleven nations you will find yourself at war with the United States." We have laid down no such principle in Asia, except as to island nations.

It is interesting to note that the British did not hesitate to use the threat of moving troops into Iran to protect their oil fields, although it would almost certainly result in bringing Russian troops into Iran, also with all the danger of a third world war.

The Russians have the same kind of a mutual-assistance treaty with Iran they have with China.

I think we have to recognize that the policy we have adopted of the containment of communism involves a constant danger that Russia may begin a third world war. But it is beyond our capacity to invade China with American soldiers, and such a program is not included in MacArthur's suggestions or anyone else's. There is no possible threat to Siberia, therefore, from anything we may do in China. On the other hand, in Europe the building up of a great army surrounding Russia from Norway to Turkey and Iran might produce a fear of the invasion of Russia or some of the satellite countries regarded by Russia as essential to the defense of Moscow. Certainly our program in Europe seems to me far more likely to produce war with Russia than anything we have done in the East. I am only asking for the same policy in the Far East as in Europe.

8. The Battle Against Communist Ideology Throughout the World

THE THREAT of communism against liberty is not by any means a purely military threat—in fact, if we had only to face the military strength of Soviet Russia I think there would not be any such concern as we see today. Communism is strong because it has developed a fanatical support and missionary ardor, which have spread throughout the world and appealed everywhere to some of those who are dissatisfied with their present condition. It is a threat because it has developed methods of infiltration and propaganda well-fitted to this missionary ardor and has succeeded in building up, even in the most free countries, at least a strong minority of people who form, in effect, a fifth column behind our lines. In France the 1951 elections showed 26 per cent of the voters to be Communists, in Italy more.

Whether we have to meet the forces of communism on the battlefield is open to question. The Russian leaders may be wholly unwilling to trust the entire future of communism to a war, in which Russia, and the Communist leaders, and perhaps communism itself, may be destroyed. They have always felt that communism has in it such elements of strength that it is bound to prevail over the system of capitalism which they denounce. They feel that capitalism has within it the seeds of its own destruction, that depression will follow depression, until the people turn to the Communist leaders for improvement in their economic conditions. They feel that the steady progress of socialism brings many countries closer and closer to the general ideals of communism. They know that socialism in the long run cannot be imposed upon a people, except by dictatorial power, and that socialism imposed by a dictatorship of a small group of enthusiasts is almost exactly the same as communism.

And so we have to consider the methods by which we can battle against the spread of communism and so weaken its spirit that its missionary ardor is destroyed. I believe that can only be done by a positive campaign in behalf of liberty. Liberty has always appealed to the minds of men and today is a far more appealing ideal than communism or material welfare can ever be. Even today I believe that a great majority of the people in the iron-curtain countries yearn for liberty against the Communistic dictatorship imposed upon them by a small minority of their own people backed by Soviet troops. In America we have clear evidence of the fact that liberty can produce the highest standard of living and the greatest happiness of any system that has ever been devised.

And when I say liberty I do not simply mean what is referred to as "free enterprise." I mean liberty of the individual to think his own thoughts and live his own life as he desires to think and to live; the liberty of the family to decide how they wish to live, what they want to eat for breakfast and for dinner, and how they wish to spend their time; liberty of a man to develop his ideas and get other people to teach those ideas, if he can convince them that they have some value to the world; liberty of every local community to decide how its children shall be educated, how its local services shall be run, and who its local leaders shall be; liberty of a man to choose his own occupation; and liberty of a man to run his own business as he thinks it ought to be run, as long as he does not interfere with the right of other people to do the same thing.

We cannot overestimate the value of this liberty of ideas and liberty of action. It is not that you or I or some industrial genius is free; it is that millions of people are free to work out their own ideas and the country is free to choose between them and adopt those which offer the most progress. I have been through hundreds of industrial plants in the last two or three years, and in every plant I find that the people running that plant feel that they have something in the way of methods or ideas or machinery that no other plant has. I have met men said to be the best machinists in the industry who have built special machines for a particular purpose in which that company is interested. Thousands of wholly free and independent thinkers are working out these ideas and have the right and ability to try them out without getting the approval of some government bureau.

You can imagine the difference between the progress under such a system and one in which the government ran every plant in the country as it runs the post offices today. There would be one idea for a hundred that are now developed. If any plant employee had an idea for progress and wrote to Washington, he probably would get back a letter referring him to Regulation No. 5201(c), which tells him exactly how this particular thing should be done, and has been done for the past fifty years. It is clear to me that the great progress made in this country, the tremendous production of our people, the productivity per man of our workmen have grown out of this liberty and the freedom to develop ideas. We have the highest standard of living, because we produce more per person than any other country in the world.

After the American Revolution and the French Revolution the whole world became convinced that liberty was the key to progress and happiness for the peoples of the world, and this theory was accepted, even in those countries where there was, in fact, no liberty. People left Europe and came to this country, not so much because of the economic conditions as because they sought a liberty which they could not find at home. But gradually this philosophy has been replaced by the idea that happiness can only be conferred upon the people by the grace of an efficient government. Only the government, it is said, has the expert knowledge necessary for the people's welfare; only the government has the power to carry out the grandiose plans so necessary in a complicated world.

Those who accept the principle of socialism, of government direction, and of government bureaucracy have a hard time battling against the ideology of communism. Our labor union leaders cannot effectively fight communism, as such, because they favor a socialist control that comes very close to communism in the actual measures which are to be undertaken. Even our statesmen seem to be handicapped in the same way. Thus, Secretary Acheson only a year ago stated: "To say that the main motive of American foreign policy was to halt the spread of communism was putting the cart before the horse. The United States was interested in stopping communism chiefly because it had become a subtle instrument of Soviet imperialism." With this point of view I emphatically disagree. I believe that we should battle the principles of communism and socialism and convince the world that true happiness lies in the establishment of a system of liberty, that communism and socialism are the very antithesis of liberalism, and that only a nation conceived in liberty can hope to bring real happiness to its people or to the world.

The first step in this campaign must be to convince ourselves and our people that we do believe in liberty and that we believe it is the solution of the world's problems. Certainly the election of 1948 was an inconclusive verdict. But in 1950 the people of this country decided that they were against socialistic plans, like the Brannan plan or socialized medicine, and that they are gradually moving toward a reaffirmation of their belief in a free system. If we can once convince ourselves that we believe in freedom, then there are many things which we can do throughout the world to meet the threat of communism.

1. We can conduct a world-wide propaganda in behalf of liberty. In the Voice of America we have already adopted the general principle of propaganda. In some places I think the

direct radio broadcast is effective, perhaps the only method of reaching the people, particularly in the iron-curtain countries. But in other countries it seems to me we should use far more local publicity organization—local radio and local newspapers. We should find those people among the citizens of each nation who agree with our principles and finance them to put on an effective propaganda. It is difficult enough for Americans to judge the manner in which propaganda should be spread in this country to obtain the support of the American people. Anybody who has run a political campaign knows the uncertainties and the weakness of any such campaign. How much more difficult is it for people sitting in America to try to judge the public opinion of Great Britain or France or Yugoslavia or Poland! The only thing that seems certain is that, however these people think, they do not think in the same terms as the American public. American publicity ideas probably will not be effective with them.

The whole propaganda question should be much more extensively studied, and it should be definitely moved away from the Department of State. The State Department inevitably is concerned with relations between nations. It does not want to do anything which might antagonize the governments with whom it deals. It wants to do things which, perhaps, will please those governments or to work out some other diplomatic purpose which it has in mind. The new agency, furthermore, should be an agency made up of men who fully believe in freedom, who concede nothing to the principle of communism, socialism, and government controls, and who believe in the cause which they are trying to promote.

2. Another method pursued by Soviet Russia is probably justified for us today under all the circumstances, although certainly it is not in accordance with American tradition and is no part of a permanent foreign policy. The Russians have developed a method of infiltration, by which they send secret agents into foreign countries, and these secret agents infiltrate every kind of organization which has some influence on the

people of the country. In this country, in particular, they undertook to get Communists into the leadership of the labor unions, into the publishing and writing fraternity, into Hollywood and the associations of actors, into the teaching profession, and into the Government itself. In these positions they undertook to make Communists if they could, but even more to influence those who were in authority to take a soft attitude toward communism. They undertook to convince them that they could use communism as a means for carrying out their ends, even though communism itself was probably not suitable to the genius of the American people. In this effort the Communists were notably successful.

This suggests, of course, that we could do the same thing, particularly in the iron-curtain satellite countries. There are many exiles from these countries who would be glad to go back. In many of the countries there is already an active underground, agitating every minute against Soviet domination. While it may be a dangerous undertaking, I believe that an able and courageous leader could successfully work out a system which would give the Soviet Government something to worry about behind the iron curtain itself. Surely, if communism can make headway in a country overwhelmingly devoted to American principles liberty should make even greater headway in a country where probably three fourths of the people prefer liberty to communism already. The OSS did work of this general character during the war. Today we hear nothing of anything being done in this field and very little being done even in the allied field of Intelligence. Our information as to what actually goes on in Russia or in the Soviet countries is of the most shadowy character.

I believe a comparatively small amount of money, if well spent, could succeed in substantially building up a love for freedom in Soviet-dominated territory, which would have a most chilling effect on any Soviet idea of military invasion of Europe and might lead to the ejection of Communist control in some of these governments. Somewhere in our Government there ought to be an agency completely advised as to the character and identity of all those forces and individuals fighting for freedom throughout the Communist world. Such an agency should be able to organize these forces to play a vital role, in war and in peace, in the ultimate undermining of the Communist conspiracy.

3. In the same general field, it seems obvious that everywhere throughout the world we should encourage and build up those forces in friendly countries or neutral countries which believe in liberty and are prepared to battle against communism. I thoroughly disapproved of the policy which abandoned Chiang Kai-shek to the tender mercies of the Chinese Communists. I have always felt that a sincere interest in the welfare of his government and a sympathetic treatment of its military needs would have enabled it to hold onto most of South China and ultimately regain control of the entire country. In Japan, in the Philippines, and in Indonesia we should be assisting and promoting those who believe in real liberty and who oppose communism. This course may lead us, in some parts of the world, toward an advocacy of the liberty of various countries which are now colonies of European nations. There is hardly a case, however, in which such liberty could not be worked out, as we worked it out in the Philippine Islands.

4. Finally, if we are going to conduct a real battle against the communist ideology throughout the world we should definitely eliminate from the Government all those who are directly or indirectly connected with the Communist organization. The American people are certainly entitled to know who it is who have been Communists and how the Communist organization is operated throughout the United States. If we are going to spend billions in battling communism in the world it seems ridiculous that we should permit secret Communist propaganda to proceed here, when we have the means of bringing it before the people. Certainly in this country it is not consistent with freedom to put a man in jail merely because he is a Communist. On the other hand, I have never seen any violation of

constitutional rights in bringing to the people's attention the fact of a man's connection with an organization and a propaganda which is clearly treasonable against the people of the United States.

In short, a war against communism in the world must finally be won in the minds of men. The hope for ultimate peace lies far more in the full exploitation of the methods I have suggested than in a third world war, which may destroy civilization itself. Far from establishing liberty throughout the world, war has actually encouraged and built up the development of dictatorships and has only restored liberty in limited areas at the cost of untold hardship, of human suffering, of death and destruction beyond the conception of our fathers. We may be able to achieve real peace in the world without passing through the fire of a third world war if we have wise leadership. Communism can be defeated by an affirmative philosophy of individual liberty, and by an even more sincere belief in liberty than the Communists have in communism. In the United States we see the product of liberty to be the greatest and most powerful nation the world has ever seen, with the happiest people. If we rise to the power of our strength, there has never been a stronger case to present to the world, or a better opportunity to dissolve its darkness into light.

Appendix

September 8, 1944

Mr. George F. Stanley, President,
The Stanley Manufacturing Company,
Dayton 1, Ohio

Dear Mr. Stanley:

I have your letter of August 31st. I am glad to give you a full statement of the course which I have pursued before the war and the actual facts relating to it.

You refer to certain information which you have gathered. All of this information is similar to that contained in a statement issued by my opponent, and like all his other statements, is inaccurate to put it mildly. The facts are as follows:

My position during the years 1939, 1940, and 1941 was based on three principles: first, that we should stay out of the war unless attacked; second, that we should build up our defense to meet any possible threat of attack; third, that we should aid Britain as much as possible, consistent with the policy of staying out of the war. This policy was exactly that professed by President Roosevelt and Wendell Willkie in the campaign of 1940, *after* the Germans had broken through in France. I did not change my mind after the election and I thoroughly disapproved of the President's persistent efforts after the election to involve us in war while professing a policy of peace. I recognize that there was a sound argument for us to enter the war, but that argument was just as sound in 1940, before the election, as it was afterwards. In fact, when Russia became involved the possible danger to this country was certainly reduced.

I may add that I have always been in favor of joining a league of nations on the theory that by joint action taken early to prevent aggression, a world war may be prevented in which we might become involved. I supported such a league in 1920 and fully agreed with the position taken by my father at that time. But it is two different things to join a cooperative organization of nations to prevent a world war, and to join in a world war after it has been brought about without our fault or participation. The only justification for entering the war was the claim that if successful Hitler would attack the United States. My own belief was that such an attack could not have been made successfully provided we built up our defense forces, and particularly our Navy. President Roosevelt himself said on January 6, 1941, "even if there were no British Navy it is not probable that any enemy would be stupid enough to attack us by landing troops in the United States from across thousands of miles of ocean, until it had acquired strategic bases from which to operate." How could those bases have been acquired if we built a navy sufficiently large? They could only have been acquired by an overwhelming superiority on the sea and in the air, such as we have acquired in the Pacific today. It would not have been acquired by Hitler.

You state that I consistently opposed all steps necessary to prepare this country for war. This is wholly incorrect. From the time I entered the Senate I voted for all appropriations for the Army, Navy, and Lend-Lease proposed by the Administration and for many not proposed by the Administration. For instance, on March 6, 1939, I voted to increase the number of airplanes authorized to 6000, of which by the way few were ordered and none delivered a year later when the Germans broke through in France. I voted for the National Defense Bill in 1939, in which Congress increased various recommendations of the President. On March 31, 1939, I voted for the bill to establish a reserve of strategic and critical materials of which little use was made by the Administration. On July 19, 1940, I voted for the bill to establish a two ocean navy. On July 19, 1940, I voted for the Army Appropriation Bill increasing the Army to 375,000, when the President had never recommended more than 225,000. On August 8, 1940, I voted to call out the National Guard, which increased the size of the Army to approximately 750,000. I voted for all the bills increasing the size of the Army and Navy, before the war and since the war started.

I did oppose the Selective Service Act of 1940, and am still opposed to the compulsory draft of men in time of peace until every voluntary method has been tried to obtain the men necessary for the force required for defense. I offered a substitute increasing the size of the Army and providing for the training of 1,500,000 men on a voluntary basis. The Navy was recruited on a voluntary basis until 1943, and it would have been easily possible to recruit by voluntary methods the number of men actually enrolled in the Army on the day of Pearl Harbor, if proper pay and allowances had been provided and a public appeal made by the President. I have always been in favor of a conscription bill in time of war or in case war is threatened and voluntary methods fail; but no real effort was ever made to recruit an army on a voluntary basis. The Army had plans to do this but never used them. The real purpose of the draft bill was to make the country war-conscious and more inclined to enter the European war.

In August, 1941, I opposed the indefinite extension of the term of draftees and National Guard when we were still at peace. The War Department's Plan and promise when the draft act was passed was that men would be taken and trained for one year and replaced by others. It proposed to build up a great reserve of men for use if war should come. As has so frequently happened since, the War Department went back on its implied promises to the men in the Army. It abandoned the whole theory of training reserves and insisted on holding on forever, even if peace continued, to those unfortunate enough to have been drafted at that time. In view of the failure of the Army to have any equipment ready for training when the men were first drafted, I proposed a substitute extending the draftees' service by six months (thus limiting peacetime service to eighteen months) and the National Guard by one year, or a total of 2½ years, providing for the training of more men. This would have carried the draft army well into the summer of 1942 and the National Guard to the end of the year, by which time a million more men could have been trained. It would have provided more trained men and more men in training at any one time than the Army's proposal. When my substitute was defeated I voted for Senator Burton's proposal to limit peacetime service to two years. I never at any time questioned or voted against the number of men stated by General Marshall to be necessary for defense.

With reference to your charge that I stated that we would never require an army of 8,200,000 men, which was General Marshall's opinion in 1943, I certainly made no such statement. In suggesting that if fathers were deferred until all others were drafted they might never have to be called, I expressed doubt as to the necessity of an army of 8,200,000. As a matter of fact, General Marshall subsequently changed his view and the Army has never exceeded 7,700,000; so that I seem to have been correct. But I never opposed giving to General Marshall all the men he asked for.

With reference to the policy of aid to Britain, I think my record is clear. As early as April, 1939, I advocated the repeal of the Arms Embargo Act on the condition that arms be exported only on a cash and carry basis, and American ships be kept out of the war zone. When proposed by the President in September, 1939, I voted for the bill to repeal the Arms Embargo and establish the cash and carry system. After the 1940 election I opposed the Lend-Lease Bill on the ground that it gave unlimited power to the President in time of peace to commit acts of war against any nation in the world. In spite of Administration protests that the Lend-Lease Bill was a peace measure, it is now finally admitted that it assured acts of war against Germany and Japan and our ultimate entrance into the war. I quote from Arthur Hays Sulzberger, editor of the New York *Times:*

"I happen to be among those who believe that we did not go to war because we were attacked at Pearl Harbor. I hold rather that we were attacked at Pearl Harbor because we had gone to war when we made the lend-lease declaration. And we took the fateful step because we knew that all we hold dear in the world was under attack and that we could not let it perish. That declaration was an affirmative act on our part and a warlike act."

At the time the President and all the advocates of the bill asserted that it was an insurance of peace, it was my opinion that we should have aided Britain by loans, and built up our production of airplanes and other armament so that they could be delivered to them in quantity. I proposed as a substitute for the Lend-Lease Bill, the power to loan two billion dollars to Great Britain, Canada and Greece. (See Congressional Record of March 8, 1941.) It was more than a year later before England obtained two billion dollars under lend-lease, so the sum I proposed was entirely adequate for the year in question. As far as aid to Britain was concerned, my substitute would have been just as effective as the Lend-Lease Act, without involving us in war. After the passage of the Lend-Lease Act and the determination of national policy thereby, I voted for all lend-lease appropriations. Once we were in the war, I thoroughly approved the policy as a means of waging war, and have twice voted to extend the Lend-Lease Act.

From March, 1941, until Pearl Harbor, I opposed all the acts of administrative foreign policy designed to involve us in the war, the seizing of Axis ships while we were supposed to be neutral, the real of the Neutrality Act sending American ships into the combat zone, and the occupation of Iceland. None of these acts had the slightest relation to the preparation of this country for war or the national defense. All of them were acts of war, and as I believe that we should not become involved in the war and that our aid to Britain should be short of war, I considered these steps unwise. They were in no sense national defense, except on the theory that national defense required our entrance into the war.

I never at any time stated that "it was fantastic to think that Japan would ever attack the United States."

You state that I said that "a Russian victory would be more dangerous to the United States than the victory of Fascism." This must be based on the following statement which I made in a radio address on June 25, 1941:

"But the victory of communism in the world outside of America would be far more dangerous to the United States from an ideological standpoint than the victory of fascism. There has never been the slightest danger that the people of this country would ever embrace bundism or nazi-ism. It is completely foreign to every idea we have learned since the nursery. But communism masquerades, often successfully under the guise of democracy, though just as alien to our real principles as nazi-ism itself. It is a greater danger to the United States because it is a false philosophy which appeals to many. Fascism is a false philosophy which appeals to very few indeed."

You will note that my reference is not to a military danger but to an ideological danger. I am quite prepared to stand by the statement that I made.

In order that you may understand my exact position on a league of nations, I herewith enclose a copy of a speech which I made over a year ago to the American Bar Association. In my willingness to abide by the decision of an international body determining a nation to be an aggressor, you may note that I go further than Secretary Hull or President Roosevelt under the plans that are now being discussed at Dumbarton Oaks.

With kindest regards,
Sincerely yours,
Robert A. Taft

RT/pr
1 enc.